J. L. Maclean

The British Railway System

J. L. Maclean

The British Railway System

ISBN/EAN: 9783744696593

Printed in Europe, USA, Canada, Australia, Japan

Cover: Foto ©ninafisch / pixelio.de

More available books at **www.hansebooks.com**

THE BRITISH
RAILWAY SYSTEM:

A DESCRIPTION OF THE

WORK PERFORMED IN THE PRINCIPAL

DEPARTMENTS.

BY

J L. MACLEAN

(CALEDONIAN RAILWAY COMPANY).

PRICE ONE SHILLING AND SIXPENCE.

LONDON:
McCORQUODALE & CO., LIMITED.
EDINBURGH:
JOHN MENZIES & CO.
GLASGOW:
McCORQUODALE & CO., LIMITED, Maxwell Street; and
WILSON & McCORMICK, 120, St. Vincent Street.

MDCCCLXXXIII.

CONTENTS

	PAGE
PREFACE	5
INTRODUCTORY	7
THE SECRETARY'S DEPARTMENT	15
THE GENERAL MANAGER'S DEPARTMENT	22
THE GOODS MANAGER'S DEPARTMENT	30
THE GENERAL SUPERINTENDENT'S DEPARTMENT	41
THE DEPARTMENT OF PERMANENT WAY AND WORKS	49
THE TELEGRAPH ENGINEER	56
THE LOCOMOTIVE DEPARTMENT	64
THE STORES DEPARTMENT	73
THE ACCOUNTANT	82
THE TRAFFIC AUDITOR	90
THE SOLICITOR	96

PREFACE.

The following chapters were contributed to the pages of the *Railway Sheet*, now the *Railway Official Gazette*. They are offered by the writer, with a deep sense of many imperfections, to his fellow-labourers in the great railway service, in the hope that they may fulfil, in some part at least, the object he had in view: namely, the setting forth in a broad, general way the duties of the officers and the staff of each of the principal departments of the railway system, and the kind of culture needful to the efficient performance of their several duties. They will have been written to little purpose if they do not encourage every young man in the service, who may honour them with a re-perusal in their revised and condensed form, to devote himself to the improvement of his position by the cultivation of his faculties in the fullest and most comprehensive sense.

The writer also hopes to find a general public curious to know something of the intricate machinery by which the work of the great nineteenth century invention of land carriage by steam is managed.

CHAPTER I.

INTRODUCTORY.

DURING the last fifty years there has been developing one of the greatest industries of which the world's history has any record. The genius of the Stephensons, and their sagacious foresight, ushered it into being and fostered it in its infancy; and they lived long enough to see it progress even beyond their hopes. From about the middle of the last century till 1825 the traffic of Great Britain was carried mainly on the canals, navigable rivers, and high roads. The invention of steam, and its application, by Arkwright, Hargreaves, Crompton, and Dr. Cartwright, to the power-loom and the spinning-mill, demanded greater facilities for the transit of coal and the raw materials of manufacture of all kinds; and also for freer, cheaper, and more frequent communication with the markets. Hitherto, nearly every industry had been cramped by prohibitive transit tariffs, and by equally prohibitive transit delays. Mr. Frederick S. Williams, in his interesting volume, " The Midland Railway: its Rise and Progress," gives the following instances of the difficulties encountered by the manufacturers in the Midland Counties up till 1839, the year of the opening of the Midland Counties Line:—" The only modes of conveyance at that time were three—the canal, the fly-waggon, and the coach—and the charges made were proportionate to the speed. Wool, for instance, required two days to travel the fifteen miles between Leicester and Market Harborough, and the expense was sixpence a hundredweight, the distance being, it was said, 'so short, and the traffic so unimportant, that they are obliged to charge an extra price.' Only three coaches ran daily each way from Leicester to Nottingham, in addition to those that passed to and from more distant points, and on which little reliance could be placed by local travellers. Similarly, many of the 'fly-waggons' were long stagers, and were of secondary benefit to the intermediate towns. Meanwhile, the charge for haberdashery, from London to Leicester, was £2 15s. a ton by canal, five shillings a hundredweight by waggon, and a penny a pound by coach." Mr. Williams observes also that " the respective conveyances were often unable to carry the quantities of goods offered. Thus, a woolstapler stated that he frequently had from 200 to 500 bags of wool lying at Bristol, which could not be brought forward by land, and he had to divide the bulk, and send it by different routes; that which went by road occupied from seven to ten days in the transit, and that by water from three weeks to a month." Among an enterprising people such a state of things was certain to call for a remedy, and everywhere over the country men were found able to suggest and carry out that remedy. The first lines of iron roads were mere tramways, intended for haulage by horse-power. The advantages these presented were that they were so laid, across country, as to shorten distance considerably; and also that, being smooth and comparatively level, they admitted of the transit of heavier freights than was possible to the "fly waggon" labouring over heavy turnpike roads. From "Whitaker's Almanack" for 1881 we learn that "the first Act obtained for the construction of a railway was that of the Surrey Iron Railway Company in 1801, for a railway from Wandsworth to Croydon. Then followed the Severn and Wye, the Berwick and Kelso, the Gloucester and Cheltenham, and other small undertakings, about twenty in number altogether, with an aggregate of 250 miles, and an authorised capital somewhat under a million." These lines were mere waggon tracks, and horses were the motive power. Although they were a distinct advance upon the older species of locomotion for goods transit, it was clear to many minds that they very inadequately met the requirements of a growing prosperity; and the first to put this into practical shape was George Stephenson, the first engineer of the first passenger railway in the world on which locomotive power was employed—the Stockton and Darlington line, which was opened on the 27th September, 1852. That day will ever be held in loving remembrance by a grateful world as the beginning of an era in the history of civilization second to none. Before leaving this short historic view of the rise of the railway system in Great Britain, let us note a few facts regarding that progress. The Stockton and Darlington line was 25 miles in length. Now, we have altogether, in the three kingdoms, 18,175 miles. That parent line cost some £200,000. Now, the aggregate capital of the United Kingdom is £831,127,312. The Stockton and Darlington Company opened with one engine. Now, we have in all some 13,727 locomotives. George Stephenson's first locomotive travelled, to his great satisfaction, at the rate of five miles an hour. Now, we have attained, on some of the great trunk lines, to a speed of 40 miles an hour. Then, the number of railway *employés* was under 300. Now, it has reached something like

325,000.* In the early days of railway enterprise capital was diffident of investing in railway property, none but those immediately interested in the development of particular districts caring to risk their means in it. Now, the general public of all ranks and classes speculate and invest in railway property to an extent, and with a confidence of results, never then dreamed of. Indeed, the development of the enterprise is affording at the present time one of the fairest channels for the profitable investment of the enormous unemployed capital of the nation. We need not stay to demonstrate that other fact, namely that the dreams even of the most sanguine as to the blessings to trade and commerce which might flow from more speedy transit of goods and minerals, have been most fully realised. The growth of production in every branch of industry has been fostered and stimulated, and the whole material wealth of the world has been cheapened simultaneously with its being brought to our very doors at command. People now travel from place to place on the slightest provocation who never moved from home before, and a journey from London to Oban, Inverness, or Thurso, is so easily performed, and with so much comfort, that thousands of tourists flock during summer and autumn to the far north and west from the busy centres of active business life, with scarcely more thought of being from home than our forefathers felt in visiting the nearest market town, and with much greater ease and safety. The great facilities which the era of railway communication has afforded the toilers in large cities of living outside their boundaries and nearer the green meadows has materially helped sanitary reform, by spreading the hitherto crowded populations over wider areas. In our forefathers' times, it is true, the population was not so large in the great industrial hives, but had railway enterprise not now existed, or had it not kept pace with industrial enterprise—a state of things we can scarcely conceive of—what would the condition of our large cities have been? Another boon which the rapid development of the railway system has conferred upon modern commercial life is the impetus it has given to a new branch of engineering, in the construction of locomotives, and also to these mechanical industries, carriage and waggon building. But for the introduction of steam locomotion, Manchester, Leeds, Crewe, Swindon, Brighton, Doncaster, and Glasgow, would have been the

---

* I am indebted to Mr. W. Fairlamb, of the Secretary's Office, North Eastern Railway, York, for these statistics, taken from his "Summary of Statistics of Railways in the United Kingdom," published in October, 1882.

poorer for the want of those extensive locomotive workshops for which they are now famous all over the globe. In short, without any pretence of being anything more than a means of offering a fair return for invested capital, the railway system is a messenger of peace to mankind, a pioneer of civilization, a mighty power for good to all. Looked at through the mists of prejudice at its inception, it has come to be a great necessity of our daily life—to many it is even daily bread itself. Some erratic Utopians, it is true, continue to regard its inroads on the country as unhallowed; but the common voice of the nation, as of all nations among whom it is developing, is in its praise, and the Utopians who would always live in an Arcadia—all their own—are allowed to scream out their anathemas unheeded.

When we speak of the progress of the railway enterprise in this country we are brought face to face with a palpable fact—one which is every day bulking more largely on our observation. There is one aspect of this great fact which does not always strike the observer, but which is well deserving of a thought. We have already said that on the railway staffs of the United Kingdom there are some three hundred thousand persons employed. What an enormous aggregate of bread-winners in a special industry—this creature of the last 56 years! The vast majority of these are the rank and file of this great army; the few are the officers holding staff appointments, and their lieutenants. The common business of these hundreds of thousands is, in its character, like no other employment. It is a special branch of industry, and requires special training in every grade to secure efficiency. In its most unskilled work it is different from all other employments, and requires *some* degree of apprehension of its special requirements; and as we ascend the scale of office, in any department, the technical difficulties increase till, the highest grades being reached, we discover that the qualities required are those of the financier, the general, the astute diplomatist, the legislator, the lawyer, or the merchant. We hope, in the chapters which follow, to prove this, and to show, in our review of the work of the principal officers, that efficient railway management requires skill of a special and a high order. When railways were in their infancy their management and working were crude, and yet from their very nature they must have presented difficulties which can scarcely now be conceived of. Men were new to the work. The officers had everything to learn. It redounds to the credit of these pioneers, however, that they successfully mastered those difficulties, and

INTRODUCTORY.

founded that great railway college in which so many have since graduated and taken honours. Until the year 1842 the working of *through* traffic —that is, traffic originating on one line and passing over one or more continuous, but separate line or lines, was cumbrous and vexatious, each company collecting its own tolls, and keeping its own accounts. In that year the late Mr. Kenneth Morrison propounded and successfully inaugurated his clearing system, by which the *foreign* or through traffic of the companies is accounted for by the terminal companies interested to the Clearing House, the companies receiving their relative proportions through that channel. A part of the clearing system also is to keep the mileage accounts of the various companies—in the matter of rolling stock of one company passing on to another territory, looking after demurrage for detention, and generally acting as standing arbitrator between them. By means of this institution of Mr. Morrison's the public, both as freighters and passengers, are saved much trouble and annoyance, in being able to book for a journey—say from Land's End to Thurso—once for all, though passing over several separate and absolutely distinct railway properties. In cases of extremity—such as those of invalids—they may even ride in the same carriage right through. The travelling public scarcely know how much they owe to the clearing system; and the railway companies have grown so much accustomed to its operations that they, also, are apt to become forgetful of the great advantage it confers. Yet there it is, performing a kind of work which could not have been performed by the companies, no matter how amicably disposed they might have been, and maintaining perfect accord among so many conflicting interests, where that seems so impossible of attainment. Once a party to the clearing system, a company knows it must abide by its decisions. Protest, when a case goes against a company, implies loss of character, and therefore of influence, when the case seems to be in that company's favour.

The railway system, then, as we have already said, is a most extensive employer of labour of a more or less skilled kind, and is always unique in the character of the work demanded. We propose to describe the work performed in the various departments; and we hope to present such a picture of the whole as to show the young cadet what may be expected of him in the department he has selected, and to offer the public an insight into the working of the varied machinery by which the carrying traffic of the country is conducted. Here we repeat that a chief reason for the publication of these papers has been to create, in the minds of the younger members of the service, such feelings of respect for the work they are performing as may help to keep up the intellectual tone of the service, and so render it still more capable of advancing the good of the nation at large.

Before entering upon our subject, we may be permitted to offer a few remarks on the general question of clerkly employment, as the departments to be described are chiefly clerkly in the character of the work required. The question has frequently been discussed, but it is growing more important day by day as the population increases, and it seems to us to deserve consideration here. It has become the fashion in modern times to regard all occupations by which the coat is soiled and the hands hardened as ungenteel, and therefore to be avoided. Many fond parents and guardians, whose sons and wards come to be disposed of, find a peculiar fascination in the idea of obtaining a place among the well-dressed gentleman-like knights of the pen for their darlings. This feeling is also shared by many young women who favour the addresses of gentlemen in broad-cloth in preference to their brethren in serge or fustian. The question which occupation pays best does not appear to vex these fond hearts much; the glory and the glitter, real or supposed, satisfy them. They pay homage to appearances, that well-known nineteenth century deity. The clerk, in olden times, was, if often poor and despised, almost always a man of learning. As learning came to be respected, the man of learning became a man in request, a member of "Society." With the march of civilization that clerical or learned order branched off into the professions of Law and the Church, with their modern sister, the Press. For the two former a somewhat strict censorship or test of fitness was found, and that has preserved them in some odour of culture, while, if no *special* scholastic test is applied to journalists, we know that only men of singular intellectual gifts succeed without considerable breadth of attainments.

Commerce, with its rapid developments and its wonderful ramifications, could not afford to wait for this thoroughness of scholarly qualifications, and seized on what it could get. Young lads just leaving school, and barely able to do more than write and cipher decently, have been, and still are, in demand for mercantile counting-houses—no tests applied. They serve the merchant's purpose, and are inexpensive. They seem to see a career before them in a calling which offers no barrier to their entrance upon it, and which accepts them and offers them emoluments at an age when their education is in reality but beginning. It is not surprising, therefore, to find that of commercial clerks the supply far exceeds the demand, and that such raw material does not often develop into anything specially superfine in the process of manufacture. The lad who has grown tired of school and its restraints and intellectual exercises, and finds companions earning wages and wearing broad-cloth, is readily seized with a longing to begin life also. If he has any real capacity he soon discovers his routine desk-work easily mastered, and, is apt to lose all stimulus to improve himself. In such a case he degenerates into a mere writer and figurer, and closes his career as a clerkly drudge. He finds nothing in his work to quicken his wits beyond the qualifications necessary to retain his desk, and he settles down into a manhood guiltless of ambition beyond newspaper-reading or gossip during his leisure hours—a very cipher in society. A new generation of youths, we are pleased to know, is being stimulated to higher ambitions by the spread of mechanics' institutions, athenæums, and evening classes for all branches of liberal culture (literary, scientific, and artistic), with the stimulus to exertion afforded by the Society of Arts' certificates awarded in the local and general examinations, and many young men are being drawn under these happy influences to the benefit of posterity.

The employment of railway clerks, as a class, is only a matter of some fifty-five years. In its present magnitude it is of daily growth. The evils which we have pointed out as existing in mercantile offices—such as perfunctory and aimless performance of duty, with no outlook towards any higher excellence—are also to be found in railway offices, but there is much less reason for such indifference in railway service. In mercantile life, unless a young man chooses to be continually changing from one employment to another, there are few opportunities for promotion. In railway life it is far otherwise. There is an infinite variety of duty and of office, and a correspondingly great variety of salary. Every clever and industrious little boy in railway service carries a possible general manager's baton in his knapsack, and, even if he fail of the first prize, the earnest lad who, without showing discontent with, or disappointment at, his present position, works with his whole heart in office, and in his leisure hours "burns the midnight oil" in study, in the endeavour to broaden his capacity for work of a higher grade, is sure of the attainment of eminence of some sort. Without this spirit of ceaseless aspiration, and the unquenchable love of working for it, there are grooves and deep ruts in the service into which the negligent and the listless are certain to sink inextricably. These latter are they whose places are easily filled; men who have mistaken their vocation, who never can hope for promotion, and all such too often sour the aspiring young souls by their invectives against an employment for which they are themselves unfit. The market is overstocked with such men. Possibly many of them would have found a more fitting sphere as mechanicians. Possibly another career would have called forth qualities which would have led to honourable position and good fortune. The first qualification for possible success is a careful selection of the most fitting career, without reference to the vulgar notion of gentility, with all its pettiness.

Again, we say, it is the purpose of these papers to incite in the young lad who has chosen a railway career, after due deliberation, an honest love for his work as part of a great scientific, commercial, and professional whole, and a determination to prepare for the highest places. If he be so fired, delay and apparent neglect will not quench his ardour—they will only add fuel to his energy. Let who will enter the service, the most capable will force their way to the front. Promotion goes by merit. No public service offers such advantages in this respect, and no service outside the Government offices makes such provision for constant employment or for old age. As a rule, as good salaries are paid by railway companies as are to be had for similar classes of work anywhere; and the advantage of permanency and provision for declining years are attractions sufficient to invite young men from commercial clerkships, where little is learned, to a branch of industry the ultimate possibilities of which are many. There is hard work in it, and long hours; but who that has health and strength, and a desire to better himself, will flinch at these? We should like to see some such test applied to aspirants for admission to railway employment of a clerkly character as the Government applies—some comprehensive examination of educational fitness. Then we should have a high class of lads offering themselves—lads well furnished, and with trained capacity, ready to receive fresh ideas and to work them out. Some of the companies apply a test of qualification, and, we believe, with some benefit. If all the companies adopted some uniform rule on this subject the intellectual quality of the service would be kept at a higher general elevation. Further—as young lads enter, seeing that they require to be trained in any case, and that their training costs the companies the time of the trainers and of the training—it might be arranged that they should be made aware of the kind of work that is performed in each department, so as to select that for which they feel best suited; and that requirement we shall endeavour to meet in the chapters which follow.

CHAPTER II.

THE SECRETARY'S DEPARTMENT.

In continuing the consideration of the subject we shall take leave to repeat our earnest desire to maintain something like fair culture among the officers of the staff, both junior and senior—culture which includes not only the basis of a good education, but implies a keen relish for the acquisition of knowledge, and the student's habit of bending the will and training the faculties. Without this the service is certain to degenerate into a vast army of possibly disciplined but unintelligent penmen and figurers, who can do as they are told, but who cannot improve upon anything they see or do. Men such as this will, and often do, pass the better portion of their lives in uninteresting drudgery, the almost mechanical routine of daily office work, unaware of anything beyond their own desks, and unfit to be entrusted with duties requiring the exercise of brains. Among this class will be found the men who grumble at untoward fortune, at slow promotion, and the difficulty of "making ends meet." We are far from saying that clever, intelligent, and thoughtful men are certain to advance in the ratio of their merits. Experience often tells a different tale. Many men whose talents point to better things are left to toil unseen, and

"Waste their fragance on the desert air."

We are equally far from alleging that fretfulness and repining are unknown among men of "parts;" but we do affirm that the really deserving are, as a class, free from noisy outcry at tardy recognition of their ability; they more frequently possess their souls in calmness, waiting, with at least the outward semblance of patience, the almost certain confidence of a coming reward. It is to this competent class that we must look for the gradual development of the service into one which the educated public will wish their sons to enter, and from which that public will look for work which will be honourable to the performers, and tend to the good of the whole commonwealth. Railway work is a great national work, and, when well done, must promote the well-being of the nation.

Turning from these general observations to the practical side of the subject, we feel it incumbent to remark that in dealing with the work of departments there is a clear duty and obvious danger. Anyone at all acquainted with railway management will appreciate both these. If our labours are to be of solid value they must indicate as clearly as possible the *general character*, without entering too much upon the *details* of the work of each office. Any attempt at showing how each company proceeds towards the working out of the same problems would overload our purpose, proving only that there are various modes of reaching the same end. In our endeavour, therefore, to open out the subject for our young recruits, we shall avoid the description of any special *system* or *practice*, contenting ourselves with a brief outline of principles, and stating the requirements of each office *generally*, so that the reader may have as broad a view of the duties required, and the qualities called for in any department, as will be equally applicable to all systems.

And, firstly, we shall look in upon the *secretary's* office. This is the principal *statutory* office. In a general way it may be said that Parliament, in passing railway bills, contemplates the need of a secretary and treasurer *only;* the former to keep the records and the registers, the latter to keep the cash. In its wisdom it has seen fit to suppose that a general management, a general superintendence, a locomotive superintendence, an engineer of the permanent way, and a goods manager, are quite unneeded for the development and working of traffic. It has nothing to say for, or of, these offices; but it clearly defines the general functions of the secretary and the treasurer. The board may appoint what other officers it needs; and the variety of these non-statutory officers which the exigencies of working has called forth on all lines will appear anon—these two, by parliamentary usage and sanction, are the only necessary departments. As the name indicates, the secretary's office implies the keeping of secrets. The incumbent must, therefore, be a non-conductor—ready to hear, but slow to speak. His staff acquire—if they are "to the manner

THE SECRETARY'S DEPARTMENT.

born"—the same faculty of unimpassioned attention, they practice reticence, which is next of kin to silence, and become adepts in diplomacy. The secretary attends all board meetings, and makes record of the business done—keeping minutes of decisions upon every question discussed. In many matters of policy and all matters of finance, he is adviser as well as recorder, and the importance of his office may be judged of by his being, with the general manager, and sometimes the solicitor, the sole custodier of undeveloped schemes long before they are ripe for hatching. To occupy a position so onerous with credit to himself and benefit to his company requires capacities which fit men for diplomacy and state-craft, and the most efficient secretary is he who combines these with a good sound knowledge of finance, which is the science and art of "making ends meet." As we write there rise before "our mind's eye" the familiar features of not a few such officers—gentlemen who confer distinction on the service by the possession of the finest qualities of head and heart and manner, and who are silently but effectively training their assistants by the influence of example no less than by precept.

The business of financing, in its most comprehensive sense, usually devolves upon the secretary personally. We do not, therefore, purpose to deal with it. There are, however, certain details which, in a greater or lesser degree, fall to the staff. Every special Act of Parliament authorising new works carries a share-creating and a borrowing power. So soon as the new works are begun, money is required for their construction, and the shareholders' sanction to raise the money—of a specified and restricted amount—is taken at a proprietors' meeting. The mode of issue of the new shares is also there resolved upon. Then begins a portion of very onerous work in the share office. Under some systems that office is administered by the secretary's staff, in others by the assistant secretary and staff, while in others it is under the superintendence of the registrar. In all cases it is under the direction and control of the secretary.

The issue of allotment letters, the receipt of these when returned with acceptance or renunciation of the shares allotted, the register of the payment of calls and issue of certificates, with the registration of all transfers of stock from one name to another, and the careful custody of the registers of proprietors—these are the duties of the share office staff, and need not be enlarged upon here. Excepting in special cases, detailed in special acts of particular companies, borrowing powers cannot be exercised by a company until the whole of the share capital has been subscribed for, and one half thereof actually paid up, and these facts must be proved before a sheriff, or other crown officer commissioned to grant a certificate; when such a certificate is obtained a company may at once proceed to issue mortgages or debenture stock to the amount stipulated in any special act. Mortgages are a terminable debenture, the rate of interest offered being in proportion to the term of years during which the mortgage runs. On the expiry of that period a mortgage may be renewed for a further period, or debenture stock may be given in exchange for it, or the money may be wanted by the lender for investment elsewhere. Debenture stock bears a fixed perpetual rate of interest. The negotiation of these loans and the correspondence which leads to the issue of that debenture stock is the work of the secretarial staff, and these demand care and precision. Sometimes this work devolves on the treasurer or cashier. Zeal without discretion in manipulating the loan and debenture stock books may easily result in over-borrowing—that is, in accepting more money than the company has power to issue bonds for; or, which is a lesser evil, will entail difficulties with the registrar's, the accountant's, and the treasurer's offices when the half-yearly balance comes to be struck. When all this responsibility is considered, it will be seen that a trustworthy and capable staff must be provided. The leading principles which regulate the negotiations must, of course, emanate from the secretary, and receive sanction of the board; but the details must be left to be worked out by the staff.

During sittings of the board and committees the secretary's office is lively. There is a constant hurrying to and fro, from board or committee room, of directors who have some one to see privately, some question to ask, some business to be transacted for them. The board has sudden need of information, or wants papers, on some subject not before thought of, and there is an exciting search for one or the other. That is to say, that sudden and unexpected demands tax the careless and undisciplined. In well organised offices, however, the junior clerks, whose duty it usually is to keep the registers of letters received and despatched, are trained to such method and regularity, that there is no confusion, no bustle—when papers are called for, whether peremptorily or more leisurely, they can readily be found. If the subject is still under correspondence, or in any way unexhausted, a reference to one special index traces them; if the matter has been finally dealt with, there is equal facility in bringing them back from their obscurity and retirement. It is the young man of some breadth of education—who is accustomed to *think*—who can be most safely entrusted with the keeping of such registers. The secret of their usefulness is in the skill shown in writing them up. The subject of a long correspondence does not always appear at a glance on the surface of the papers; it may have to be searched for, and when found may be capable of a variety of settings, according to one's particular point of view. To *know* what the subject is, and to be able to turn it over and over, and see it from everybody's standpoint, and so to register it, that any one of a variety of people looking for it under his own heading, might find the papers, is not an easy task, nor one to be despised as menial. Compared with the duty of merely writing letters to dictation the register keeper's is highly intellectual.

With the growth of the railway system, the work of the departments has greatly increased, and in many cases it would scarcely be possible to overtake all that has to be done without the aid of shorthand. With its help the heads of departments and their principal assistants are enabled to compress the routine work of an office within the early hours of the day, leaving them leisure to overlook the working-out of detail, to make new and cancel old systems of working as circumstances suggest, to meet inquirers, &c. An educated youth, accustomed, as we have said, to think for himself, is of infinite value in all the principal offices of the service; but in none more than in the secretary's, in this respect, that, except on very important occasions, when the turning of a phrase in a letter, or an official document, may be the touchstone of the company's policy, and the fullest and maturest experience must be called in to advise, he may safely be left, with a simple hint of what is to be said, to amplify it, in the most suitable words, in correspondence. To those who have much letter-writing to do, along with other routine office work, the great advantage of such intelligent help as that must be evident. There is, in such cases, no need to dictate verbatim all we would say; and what a saving of time that implies! In the exercise of such faculties as this art of letter-writing then, our youth have excellent opportunities of improvement in the department under consideration. They must learn the wisdom of those words of Robert Burns—

"Aye free, aff han' your story tell,
When wi' a bosom cronie,
Yet still keep something tae ye'rsel
Ye'd scarcely tell tae ony."

With practice, they acquire the ability to weigh the niceties of meaning between synonymous terms, and to guard against the chance of being misunderstood. If a youth on entering this important department of the service has not already graduated in grammar in its higher developments in analysis, and *precis* writing, he cannot better equip himself than by a course of such study. By means of the mental power which such culture imparts, our youth can be trained for the highest offices, with the fullest confidence of success. Without it they will never be anything but indifferent copying clerks. If, in starting upon their career, they are capable of seizing upon the root-subject of a long correspondence, where no distinctive title appears, and setting it clearly down in a variety of forms, on as many different pages of a letter index or register for future reference, or of "boiling down" the contents of that correspondence into the form of a *precis*, they give token of the possession of faculties requiring scope for their excercise, and are invaluable.

A most important function of the secretary's office is the drafting of minutes of the meetings of the board, the committees, and the proprietors. Some of these are routine, many are only a remove above routine, but the most numerous require care, and some literary skill, as, apart from the need to be accurate as to fact, about which the board before passing them are sure to be critical, there is always, to a man of cultivated tastes, a desire to crystallise his thoughts into their compactest form. The staff have no responsibility in this matter, excepting always the assistant secretary, who does duty at one or other of the committee meetings, and who, therefore, drafts his own minutes. If, however, the staff are not required to draft minutes, they have occasion to read them, and to issue extracts from them to those whom they concern, and the stamp of young assistants we have just been commending are most unlikely to allow such an educational process to pass unimproved.

Stock certificates are signed by or for the secretary; mortgage bonds, debenture stock certificates, agreements, and nearly all manner of deeds to which the company is a party, must also be signed by him. These signatures devolve no care or trouble on his clerks however.

Half-yearly and extraordinary general meetings are a great test of the value of the secretary's staff. The issue of the half-yearly report and statement of accounts is left to them, the accountant and the auditors with the secretary and the board having first decided upon the proper charges to revenue or capital on all debateable questions, and resolved upon the dividend to be recommended. From the time of issue of this statutory document, which must take place within eight days of the half-yearly meeting, until after that meeting is held, shareholders, both male and female, write or call " wanting to know, you know," why this is thus, or curious to have an explanation of some difficulty. It need not be wondered at if ladies find cause for such inquiry, since gentlemen, otherwise clever and experienced in accounts, think it necessary, as so many do, to show their careless glance at the items of charge and discharge, by putting questions which, in the light of the accounts, require no answer, but a simple reference to the document itself. At such a time the secretary's staff need have temper in complete subjection, and the faculty of "turning away wrath" with "a soft answer." And *that* we take it is a considerable part of the special drill of the department. Under a chief whose manner is courteous and obliging the infection of manner is catching, and works wonders upon proprietors of a troublesome and fault-finding disposition. Though there is a natural inclination to consider inquirers as nuisances, the fact remains that they have a *right* to inquire, and also a *right* to expect fair civility in meeting them. It is, at all times, a mark of the absence of true culture to exhibit temper, and he who has a natural tendency to feel *annoyed* has a discipline to undergo which is of the greatest possible value—if he would only see it in that light. The half-yearly meeting time is, therefore, even when dividends are good, a trial to some, and an education to all. The secretary's office is, as a rule, the chief of the in-door or book-keeping, as the general manager's is of the out-door or traffic department.

In this hasty glance at the secretarial section of the subject, we have tried to indicate something of the nature of the work done in that office as a general rule. We are aware that few secretary's assistants may find an exact transcript of their own office work in our description. We believe, however, we have embraced the most general items of duty performed in the aggregate.

We have now to offer a few words of advice to aspirants for honour in the department. There is such need for a careful and educated literary style, for clear apprehension, for quick and vivid perception, if the aspirant would render efficient service, command attention, and deserve promotion, that we think those who give no promise of these mental qualities, and have failed to acquire the necessary style, should be deterred from entering upon an unsuitable career. To those who have any leaning towards the work, a desire to acquire the needful culture, or having passed fairly forward in a generous education, are attracted to the duties of the office, for the opening they offer to an honourable career, in which there are occasional prizes worthy of men of high intelligence, we say, look onward hopefully, cultivating the graces of a well-balanced and gradually ripening intellect by the study of English literature and history, current history—the higher arithmetic and algebra will be found extremely useful—a little French or German, and a little law. Such knowledge of the latter as is needful may be easily attained by careful reading and annotation of any of the best authenticated digests with which the press now teems. If this seems at all a severe course of training for the efficient discharge of the duties of the secretarial department, we submit it will only appear so to those who lack the qualification for advancement in the office, for the really capable are just those who will regard such difficulties as so many stepping stones to success.

CHAPTER III.

THE GENERAL MANAGER'S DEPARTMENT.

THE general manager is the company's chief administrator. Equally with the secretary, he sits at all board meetings to advise. His opinions are always needful to the direction in matters affecting the policy of the company, in its relations with its competitors, and in the development of its resources. To be successful he must be a man of vigorous intellect and of active habits, and should combine firmness of purpose with the grace of a conciliatory spirit. In his administrative capacity these invaluable qualities are inestimable. The officers and servants under his command, with various capacities and endowments, and with infinite shades of disposition, must ever, even in the most exceptional circumstances, be a source of worry to the manager; but that difficulty may be greatly mitigated if the office is held by a man who has the gift of *persuasion*.

THE GENERAL MANAGER'S DEPARTMENT.

Autocratic rule is neither pleasant nor profitable; and it surely tends to degenerate the staff. If officers or servants feel that the will which governs them is unsympathising, unflinching, quick to punish, and slow to commend, a doubtful and half-hearted obedience is the result; and resignation in disgust is the almost certain corollary. In the army and navy, where implicit, unquestioning obedience is necessary to discipline, and where the nature and conditions of the service render breach of discipline a punishable offence, the superior officer who wields his authority with humanity and kindness compels a superior order of obedience to his will, and commands respect instead of fear. If, then, it has been ascertained and established in such autocratic services as those of the army and navy, that *popular* rule, with needful firmness, is the best, how much more necessary is it in a voluntary service like the railway service that the management should be entrusted to those who have the power to *attract* as well as command. It requires little demonstration to prove that a constantly changing staff cannot be an *efficient* one; and that harshness and implacability are almost certain to produce dissatisfaction and desertion.

The office of general manager, to be efficiently discharged, requires certain attainments and certain gifts in the incumbent. The gifts are: this power to administer without severity to which we have alluded; a genial address—the outcome of a pleasant disposition; a clear brain— apt to perceive and to generalise from complicated details; and ready and persuasive speech. The quality of good address is needful in the numerous negotiations in which a manager is certain to be engaged with traders, public corporations, &c., and a conciliatory spirit conquers opposition and secures easy terms. Unclouded brains command respect everywhere; but nowhere more certainly than in positions of power and responsibility such as that of the ruling spirit of a great railway company. "Time is money" to the trading classes, and to the hard-wrought railway officer; and the man who is quick to apprehend all the intricacies of every project which is submitted for his consideration, is a most valuable, or rather invaluable, acquisition to a company with much important work to do. Persuasive speech works wonders in the board-room, and in more private, but not less important, consultation with the departmental heads, with deputations of the travelling public with grievances to redress, or with the thousand-and-one outsiders who want things their own way, and mean to have them. In such cases the power to say "No," and yet send his "deputations" and other troublesome and time-killing visitors away as well pleased as if he said "Yes," is a gift of the highest order in a general manager. Such a man can make his demands upon a cheese-paring or short-sighted directorate with the almost certainty of having his own way, and may thus be at once a powerful advocate for his staff and the truest friend of his company. The attainments which should distinguish such an officer are those which he has acquired while graduating in more humble office. Having an efficient body-guard of officers in charge of the departments, each fitly furnished in his own sphere, it is not required that he should have exact knowledge of the working out of detail in each. He will generally be found to know enough of all, however, to be able to sympathise with the difficulties of each, and to be consulted with intelligence in emergency; and he will, moreover, while taking an independent view of each case which is submitted for judgment, be ready to set a proper value upon the opinion and advice of the officer consulting him. The responsibility of his office—he being, with the secretary and solicitor, a custodian of the company's unpublished policy—makes him reticent and cautious, and he finds it prudent on occasion, to practice the virtue, the *golden* virtue, of *silence*. To a man who must necessarily mix much with public men, and is thus liable to insidious and specious flank movements to reach the whole truth of his company's intentions, this must be a trying ordeal, and he who has acquired the art of so answering such attacks as to cover his own retreat without giving anything up has graduated in a good school. We can remember some general managers, of a past age, who carried this to the verge of secretiveness, keeping even their brother officers in ignorance of the "reason why" in issuing their manifestoes. That this was a mistake we need not stay to prove. An intimate acquaintance with the system of railways, sidings, canals, depots, &c., placed under his charge, if not absolutely necessary, is, at least, of great importance to the general manager, who, by such knowledge is able at all times to judge for himself more readily in cases affecting the working of traffic which may be submitted for consideration. Something of the nature of an acquaintance with the special traffic or produce of each district is useful to him who has its transit to regulate and provide for, although the departmental officers may be presumed to make that a special study, and to be able to advise him. Next to this branch of information, which the manager of inquiring habit is certain to cultivate, is a somewhat similar acquaintance with the character and products of his neighbour's territory, and specially with the points of junction with his company's lines; and this will occasionally lead him to the projection of fresh feeders, *now* into untrodden regions lying into his own lines, *then* into unthought-of corners of his neighbour's ground. The former is easy, comparatively, and, if conceived in a generous spirit, is certain to receive support from the district to be traversed, if not from the board. The latter requires *finesse*, to carry conviction to those proposed to be scheduled for land or "amenity," and to keep the secret of the intended invasion from the company in possession until they have no other resource than to oppose the bill in Parliament. When his project reaches that stage, and the decision of a committee of Parliament is solicited, the general manager of the highest order of capacity and attainment finds his favourite arena. He surrounds himself with his most trusted witnesses, has his confidential consultations with counsel, arranges his evidence, and waits his turn to be examined. In the witness-box he yields himself to a careful and well-prepared examination in chief, cautiously fencing in cross, and offering nothing but what is extorted from him. During the hearing of evidence for the opposition he is untiring in his watchfulness, prompting questions and calling attention to the joints in the enemy's armour at which to point attack. At this time his evenings in the vicinity of Westminster are devoted to consultation, or to preparation for the next day's campaign and the arrangements needful for success. If our general managers are highly-paid officers they are not "the right men in the right place" if they do not deserve it. They sleep not on beds of roses, nor often leave official cares behind them when they lock up their cabinets and betake them to the family dinner-table and the quiet joys of home. We know of no class of men so weighted with heavy responsibilities, and we are pleased to think that the railway service has reared so many whose qualities are statesmanlike, and who are worthy of the highest honours in the gift of the Crown. We have endeavoured, we fear very inadequately, to describe them and a few of their functions and responsibilities, and to hold them and their high office before the eyes of the young as deserving of their highest regard, and of their most careful imitation. The general managers of the future are in our offices, cultivating their faculties, and acquiring knowledge and experience. Let them look around them and above them for living examples of what they ought to be.

Now, we shall see what kind of work the general manager requires of his office staff; and on this subject we have again to explain that it is not our intention to picture any *one* office, but to give as comprehensive a sketch of the requirements of the office generally as may include the whole. We may begin this section of the subject with the observation that on some of the most extensive systems the service of an *assistant* manager is required. To that officer the general manager relegates a portion of the details of management. As, however, the assistant manager's duties are, practically, the manager's, we need not dwell upon them separately, satisfying ourselves with this one remark, all the more needful here that we have not mentioned it in speaking of the manager —that the assistant frequently takes the place of the manager at the quarterly and other meetings at the Clearing House and elsewhere. Our readers will be aware that Clearing House business is regulated by committees of the traffic officers of the various companies—the general managers, the goods managers, and the superintendents, who sit once a quarter in the Clearing House premises, Seymour Street, Euston, London, and in the case of Ireland, in the Clearing House premises, Kildare Street, Dublin. The two latter classes of officers sit in the same week on separate days, the former a few weeks later, to revise and approve the minutes of their proceedings. To be a thoroughly competent assistant manager, then—that is, one who, upon occasion, can take up any of the manager's functions, and fulfil them satisfactorily—requires abilities and qualifications of the same order, and the subordinate office is frequently the stepping stone to the superior. Besides the assistant manager, there is, necessarily, a *principal assistant*, whose duty is to regulate the office work, distributing it among the members of his staff, and having a general oversight of its performance. This post is usually held by a junior officer of some experience and educational qualifications—one who may be trusted to apprehend clearly and rapidly what is wanted from a few general hints, and who possesses tact, manner, method, and arrangement. He is the manager's right hand, knows everything, hears everything, has a place for everything, and is unfailing in readiness and accuracy. The manager's time is constantly occupied, and is, therefore, of great value. People call for him. Some *must* see him. A clever tactician will readily discern whether they *ought* to see him, and act accordingly, without giving offence. Directors' meetings for special traffic purposes are sitting, deputations of traders, or of daily travellers, have audience at pre-arranged times, or the manager calls the departmental officers together in conference. On all these and similar occasions the principal assistant arranges the business, and has all needful papers at hand. In order to be always ready, this officer must have a capable and orderly staff; but he must know everything himself. He must often be his own index to everything in the office, and that can only be achieved by having "a place for everything, and everything in its place;" and by training his juniors to habits of method and orderliness. He should command the respect of those placed under him by the thoroughness of his knowledge, and will find it lessens his difficulties if he secures their esteem by amiability of temper and disposition. He should add to practical skill in the discharge of his official duties the graces of as broad culture as possible, as the whole *tone* of the office will probably be influenced by his example. In the hands of a really capable, clever, and amiable man, this important office may be administered with incalculable benefit to a wide circle of the young and the impressionable in the ranks.

The working staff of the manager's office should be, like the secretary's staff, fairly, if not liberally, educated. They should also, looking to future promotion, be studious in their habits, occupying their leisure in building up and strengthening the fabric of their earlier education. None of us know too much, even in our present spheres, and we cannot predict what may be required of us, or what tests applied to us in the future when promotion offers. The youth who, on leaving school or college, throws aside his books with a relish, and never looks at them again, will never be anything but a machine, a *mechanical clerk*, destined to be governed, never to hold the reins. Next to this general culture, this yearning after improvement, every clerk in a general manager's office should be a shorthand writer. The enormous quantity and the quality of the work devolving upon the manager, and upon the principal assistant render it necessary to employ shorthand to save time. The manager frequently dictates important letters and papers in rapid succession to a shorthand clerk for immediate transcription and signature, and the principal assistant would rarely get along without similar aid. In many of the greater services the directors have established classes for instruction in the art, at the company's cost. Where that has not been done, however, earnest lads will be able to help themselves and each other by the use of Mr. Pitman's most excellent books. A neat and swift handwriting, and a taste for making out statements, are also needful qualifications for a desk in the general manager's office; while a fair acquaintance with arithmetic, and, as we have already shown, a disposition towards orderliness and method are indispensable.

The youngest members of the staff learn to use the copying-press, and are taught how to copy neatly and clearly, and to take *double* impressions. These latter, they learn, are required to complete the regular sequence of correspondence which has to be filed past. They also learn to keep the index and the journal of letters received. In our last chapter we indicated *how* the index should be kept to be really useful and ready when wanted. The *journal* is a book in which every letter, every document coming into the office should be entered as received. Opposite each entry in this book—where such a book is kept—is a consecutive or running number which, with the date, is either stamped or marked upon the document before it is dealt with by the principal assistant. Whatever is done with that document, if it leaves the office, is recorded in the journal, and we may say that the careful and accurate keeping of that book saves much time and vexation. We are aware that the practice of the companies varies greatly as to this book—some of them relegating it to the office-keeper's department, and leaving the duty of keeping it for *all* departments to one person. That system is not, however, so extensively practised as that which we have described. The reports of accidents on the line, in the workshops, on the station platforms, etc., involving loss of, or injury to, life, either of passenger or official, damage to plant or machinery, etc., are sent by the heads of the departments interested to the general manager, who deals with the men who caused them, summarily, if the offence or consequence is trifling, or by submitting the matter, after official investigation, to the directors for their decision. The Board of Trade has supplied a form for reporting *all* accidents, of whatever kind, to "the Lords of the Privy Council for Trade," and it is the duty of certain members of the manager's staff to make these reports. In acknowledging receipt of these documents, the Board of Trade intimate having appointed one of their inspectors—naming him—if they think the accident worthy of inquiry, and asking that suitable arrangements may be made for his gaining access to the place, and to the men involved. By the time the Board of Trade issues its report, after this inquiry, the papers on the subject in the manager's office are voluminous, including the reports of the company's own officers, and the correspondence passing between these, and between the Board of Trade and the manager. That correspondence, equally with all other sets of correspondence and masses of documents, should pass through the index to be easily accessible. In the case of damage to goods in these accidents, the matter of settlement of claims is left with the goods manager; but where passengers have been injured, the arrangement of compensation questions is by one company left to a special officer, attached to no particular department; by another to some member of the general manager's staff, while in other cases the secretary or the solicitor, or assistant secretary, has charge of the arrangements. While the initiative in train arrangements, and the making up of the company's time tables, is taken by the general superintendent and the goods manager, the general manager is, in all changes, consulted, and his sanction has to be obtained before the arrangements can be carried into effect. This, however, devolves no work upon the manager's staff, and we mention it merely as an item of the managerial responsibility. All agreements with traders and others emanating from the manager, his principal assistant and staff require to keep these numerous and varied documents carefully arranged and docqueted, if not, indeed, as is most frequently done, posted up in books prepared for the purpose. These are so often wanted for reference that accurate and full indexing is indispensable, and the most painstaking, methodical, and intelligent members of the staff are usually detailed to this duty, and also to the work of seeing that the company's Acts of Parliament are at all times set in order. A young man anxious to become useful will do well to make himself familiar with the special provisions of each Act and its date, and that acquaintance can readily be acquired by a little occasional reading and a few notes. The general manager, with so many constantly changing distractions, cannot be expected to remember every detail; so that such special knowledge as this must prove a young officer's interest in his work, his aptitude, and his thoughtfulness, and be of incalculable service to his chief.

Reports are sent to the general manager by the superintendent of the locomotive department from time to time of the depreciation of rolling stock, and the necessity for renewals, repairs, and additions, together with regular statements showing cost of locomotive working, train mileage, &c.; by the resident engineer of the condition of the line under special weather conditions, such as floods, frosts, snow storms, &c., and calling attention to the need for special powers to meet special emergencies. The general superintendent or the telegraph superintendent reports proposed alterations or additions to the block-signalling arrangements, and to the company's telegraph wires. The stores superintendent complains that the departments cannot use certain material which he has had instructions to order for them. The goods manager reports deviation of traffic by a competing company, and produces a mass of correspodence to prove that the enemy has stolen a surreptitious march. The company's superintendent of horse presents a black list of deaths in the stalls, on the streets, or in the " convalescent home." Everybody reports to the general manager, whose staff must, if they are equal to their positions, learn to lessen his burthens, and help him to overtake everything by *earnest, intelligent, prompt,* and *united* action.

CHAPTER IV.

THE GOODS MANAGER'S DEPARTMENT.

THE goods manager is, *facile princeps,* the chief traffic manager, for, while railway companies are expected by their obligations to Parliament and the public to provide for the comfortable and safe transit of Her Majesty, Her Majesty's lieges, and the respected " foreigner," every one knows, and those interested in railway property better than any, that goods and mineral traffic pay best, and are, therefore, the chief sources of a company's revenue. They require no first-class accommodation, with warming-pans; no sleeping and drawing-room saloon cars; no first-class waiting-rooms; no elegantly equipped station superintendents; no expensive, illuminated posters, to invite or attract them; and no flying squadron of ticket collectors to intercept them at unexpected stations with " Tickets, please!" Excepting in the case of live stock, which also comes under the goods manager's care, there is no need of " cleaners." Live stock trucks, it is true, require washing out and disinfecting after every trip, as do the cattle pens and sidings, but goods waggons and vans, and mineral trucks, demand no attention except the inspection of wheels, axles, and buffers for the safety of the line. If goods are " soft," or seriously damageable by water, they require stowage in covered vans if less susceptible to injury by the elements, they ungrumblingly put up with open waggons, and are content, even in mid-winter, with a waterproof sheet tied over them. They pay fair freights, and yet never complain of travelling in mixed company, and are as well pleased to make a long journey among straw or sawdust as if they had lain upon handsome Brussels rugs, with the company's crest or initials wrought into them. And, lastly, it seldom matters, except in the case of ill-natured, short-grained castings, whether the buffers are "dead" or "spring," whether the couplings are tight or loose, or the bearing-springs easy or rigid. The traffic, as a rule, comes out at the end of the journey looking marvellously fresh—much fresher, indeed, than the man who consigned the merchandise would be likely to appear after a similar amount of travel under circumstances so much more costly to the carrying company. All this is to say that, earning in many cases—nay, indeed, in nearly all—more revenue, at infinitely less cost, the goods and mineral traffic is the most important to the carriers, and, therefore, the *first* in value to the companies.

Unlike the general manager, the goods manager is purely an administrator. Receiving instructions from the general manager, or direct from the board, he sets all the machinery of his department moving to perform their behests. We have said there were, at the initiation of railways, pioneers, who had to form their own precedents and to invent their own machinery. The systems they inaugurated have done splendid service, and there still are traces of these in the *modus operandi* of modern management.

The half century of railway life which has passed since steam locomotion became a fact has, however, created new wants, laid bare the defects and deficiencies of original methods, and offered scope for the thoughtful teaching of experience, of which ample advantage has been taken. The mantle of the pioneers has fallen upon the shoulders of capable men who have benefited by experience, and who have been founding a college of instruction in railway science most invaluable to their young successors. The present generation of goods managers has almost entirely graduated in this school, and its constituent members are, all unconsciously, the professors of a later school. Their assistants, of all grades, are silently but effectively catching inspiration and deducing lessons from their conduct of affairs; and thus, year by year, the solid fabric of a noble public institution is growing towards greater usefulness and higher perfection. These remarks apply to all departments of the service, but they seem to us specially appropriate when considering the goods manager and his office.

In administering his office as chief of the goods, mineral, and live stock departments, the goods manager, it will readily be understood, has heavy responsibility. It is true, he must be, and is, assisted by a staff of junior officers with sectional oversight, but that very division and subdivision of responsibility increases his own—for that is always best done which we do ourselves. This feeling of anxiety as to everything being done as he wishes, together with the constant reference to him for advice or instruction in difficulty, and the hindrance to exhaustive consideration of the various subjects with which he must deal personally, are a serious strain upon the physical power of the man. He had, therefore, needs begin with robust health and temperate habits. If he adds to these those other almost indispensable gifts, activity and energy, much of the worry which wears out the nervous system will be avoided, as work disappears rapidly before both, and bores and stupids learn to respect his estimate of the value of time. It is amazing how little provocation some people require to induce them to intrude upon a busy man's time, and how difficult it is to awaken them to a sense of their thoughtlessness. We have known men of the rarest sweetness of disposition tried most severely in this way, and have admired the grace of manner with which their tormentors have been received; but we have frequently thought that a little wholesome gruffness would have prevented repetition of the offence. There can be no doubt, however, that a kindly, courteous, and amiable temperament illuminates intellectual gifts, and elevates its possessor supremely above his fellows. In railway work of any kind it is extremely difficult to cultivate this; but it is always desirable to aim at it. Among personal qualifications for the high office of goods manager, one of the chief is that of a good address. He has to urge his views upon the acceptance of the board, or to defend his administration before them, to explain his company's policy with reticent caution at conferences, to excuse his company to angry traders in cases of neglect of their wishes, or when compelled to say "no" to their demands; possibly all the while conscious of offending either, or all. Clear views, fulness of knowledge, quickness of perception and apprehension, and the activity and energy to which we have alluded, are the characteristics of the best of our goods managers. Some of these are gifts, and may not be bought, in their highest excellence, by practice or experience. We think, however, that much headway in all may be made by even dull men, *willing* to attain to the highest perfection, and—*trying*.

These observations are directed to the foundations of the intellectual character of the man, according to our estimate of his needful culture, and he who possesses these, in any degree, will easily overcome all other difficulties of his office. That is to say, such a man may have been trained for his profession in *any* of the services, and his knowledge of details may be local to the particular system or line of railway on which he graduated. He may have spent many years in his first school, and its system may seem to colour his forms of thought—for there is infinite *variety* in the *unity* of the modes of working out in detail among the companies—yet, if he is transplanted from one company's service to another, he readily masters the little geographical differences. To serve a high railway office after this fashion, and with such capacities is to bend the faculties to the will, and is an important factor in that *culture* after which we should like to see our youth striving. It is the distinguishing glory of our profession, among all but the most learned—and, indeed, it is little if anything behind these—that the greatest rank is not to be deservedly attained in it without the cultivation of the highest intellectual gifts. Comprehensiveness, clearness, readiness, discrimination, decision, and firmness—the capacity of *thought*, concentrative, yet easily diverted, without loss of concentration, to a thousand and one grave responsibilities. If a young man enters the service with the full knowledge of such lofty purpose and possibility in his career, he will only require *opportunity*, and even if opportunity comes not, or arrives too late for long enjoyment, he will have his reward in a higher enjoyment of what he has.

An essential to good management is a full and accurate knowledge of the geographical position of the particular company's lines and branches, with a fair acquaintance with those of neighbouring and competing companies. Allied to this, there should be a careful study of the products of each district, its mineral, agricultural, and manufacturing wealth, and the markets for these; also some attention to the needs of the population living in the districts served by the lines, and the sources of their supply, will be found useful. Whenever opportunity offers, the same kind of study of a neighbouring company's territory, its possibilities and requirements, should prove beneficial, because, apart from aggressive or competing measures which such knowledge may foster, each company may be helpful to the other in fair barter of traffic. Next to an acquaintance with the districts over which he rules, the goods manager must possess some knowledge of the various classes and scales of rates scheduled in his company's special Acts of Parliament, without which he would not be able to encourage trade over his lines. In these Acts Parliament gives the company certain powers to levy tolls upon all kinds of traffic, classifying it, and restricting the company to a maximum rate in each class. In fixing these rates Parliament had in view the cost of *working* the traffic; and it is not often that the maximum rate in any class is found unremunerative. Indeed, we may say that perhaps none would be more blameworthy in such an event than the company themselves, since the various rates scheduled are their own figures, or at least agreed to by them in pressing for their bill. It is not always expedient, even where there is no competition, to charge the maximum rate; and, when competition steps in to share the chances of the traffic, it is often found necessary to reduce an already existing rate. Rates are also frequently modified to encourage a larger traffic, or because a large traffic, like a large wholesale order, demands a wholesale rate. The goods manager must know something of the cost of working—what it takes to make locomotive, waggon, and waggon-cover earn their right to exist. With such data, and a consideration of the mileage and the work required in handling the goods at each end of the journey, he is in a position to say how much less than the highest rate allowed he may fix with a fair profit to the company, and a hope of encouraging traffic. So far as purely *local* traffic—that is traffic passing from one station to another of the same company's territory—so long as neither station is in a town in which a neighbouring company has a footing—is concerned, the goods manager is his own arbiter—within the limits of his company's powers. If, however, the traffic is to pass to a town common to two or more companies, although it is sent from one to another station of the same company's system, the rate asked for can only be adopted on all the companies interested agreeing; the company taking the initiative completing the arrangements for the formal adoption and issue of the rate. In such cases—as in all matters affecting the interests of more than his own company—the goods manager has an excellent guide in the "Clearing House Regulations," a little book published annually by that most wonderful product of the railway system, the "Railway Clearing House." That little manual, every year growing more bulky, contains the essence of all he ought to know with regard to the interchange of traffic and the rights of competition; and it is essential that he should be master of its leading principles—his assistants, in their several departments, will keep him right on points of detail.

In virtue of his office this gentleman is a member of the Goods Managers' Conference, which sits in London, in the Clearing House premises, periodically, for the discussion of all questions affecting the general railway traffic of the country. England and Scotland are represented in the institution in Seymour Street, London, while Irish business is transacted—as we have already indicated—after the same, or a nearly similar form, at the Irish Railway Clearing House in Kildare Street, Dublin. In the intervals of the meetings negotiations as to alterations in rates may be carried on with the companies interested. Prior to each meeting the companies supply the Clearing House with a list of subjects which they propose to submit for discussion, and,' in return, the goods managers are furnished with a printed copy of the agenda, or list of subjects to be brought before the meeting by the various companies, with the names of the proposers attached, so that each knows his neighbours' proposals, and goes up prepared to discuss them. This necessity for attending the periodical meetings tests the quality and fibre of the man; and, according as he conducts his business, in urging the acceptance of his own suggestions, or criticising those of others, he makes or mars his *legislative*, his *only* legislative, reputation. He is also, in virtue of his office, liable to be appointed upon the Claims Arbitration Committee, which sits in the same premises, and is in session in the same week. This committee decides in all disputed claims between the companies interested, and also in cases of claims paid in alleged infringement of Clearing House rule, to make favour with traders in the hope of securing traffic from a competing route. The decision of the conference and committee are final and binding after they have passed the revising tribunals of the General Managers' Conference, the Clearing House Committee—consisting of delegates from the various boards—and has received the approval of those boards.

Some skill in arranging trains, and in the distribution of plant, is also called for in a model goods manager, although, so far as the latter is concerned, most of the companies have a responsible officer detailed to the duty, who has a *quasi* independent position, always, of course, subject to the command of the goods manager, who alone can know where plant, either goods, mineral, or live-stock, is most in demand. If not indispensable, it is a material advantage to the goods manager to have some slight general knowledge of manufactured goods, as he will then be in a position to judge of the fairness of claims made for their value when damaged—a most important function to exercise. This knowledge, like much else which an energetic man accumulates in his path through life, may be acquired by habits of observation, and the constant use of the faculty which is ceaselessly inquiring. We do not promise that by such a process he can become a *merchant* or *manufacturer*; but we do say that he will learn as much of many articles of manufacture, many products of the loom, as will often enable him to put the manufacturer to rout in cross-examination. He should have same practical experience of accounts, in order to be able to see clearly and rapidly where it is needful to call the special attention of the traffic auditor, or audit accountant, to the examination of station accounts. And it is almost an indispensable characteristic of the goods manager that he should have the faculty of discerning character; without this he cannot well trust himself in the selection of his staff.

If the picture we have drawn be a fair one—and we leave it to our more advanced readers to say whether they cannot apply the leading features to men of their acquaintance in the railway service—may we not proudly hold the portrait before the eyes of our young friends as examples of what they may become by efficient study, and as incitements to the attainment of such possible capacity? He who aims at the moon may shoot one of the stars.

A goods manager, be he ever so capable, is like a great general without a well-selected and well-appointed staff, if he is not flanked by capable assistants. And every able man will feel his ability increased rather than lessened by the consciousness of having a body-guard of young officers of education and attainments at his command on every occasion. He must have some one particular assistant, who is ready and able to take his place in his frequent absence. If such an officer is carefully selected, he will manifest most of the qualifications of his chief, in being conversant with the wants of the traffic on the line, and the best means of fostering it. He will have good address, be at home among the

Clearing House rules, will be "guide, philosopher, and friend" of the subordinate heads of departments in all matters of difficulty, and have discretion enough to know when to yield a point for policy-sake. Having the office staff under control, and the responsibility of the official machinery working smoothly resting upon him, he will discover in his management, the happy blending of firmness with suavity, of "justice tempered with mercy." He will be a good correspondent, a man of rapidity of thought, and of decision of character, be methodical in habit, and a good supervisor and administrator. With respect to the staff of the goods manager's office, there is probably as great diversity in the mode of distribution of the work as in the style of its performance among the companies. We can only indicate, therefore, such general features as are common to all. "Rates" and "general correspondence" are the principal divisions, the latter including everything not comprised in the former. The head of each of these divisions should be a capable administrator, and he should chiefly be a *specialist* in all that concerns his own department most particularly. The really efficient chief-rates clerk knows his company's parliamentary limits and obligations, and those also imposed by the Clearing House; and if a new rate is wanted, or a modification of an old one is desired, *he* is the man to apply to. His books would form a fair library in the number of the volumes, but they would be liable to be neglected by the "general reader." The constant changes to which rates are subject, and the enormous variety of them, must render it, even to him who has to do with these changes, an almost perplexing puzzle to say which is the correct rate in any case. How much more perplexing must quotation of one, in answer to the inquiry of a trader, be to the novice! Changes are not merely numerous, they are in some instances frequent, and unless every one of them is carefully engrossed, quotation is difficult, and reference to the book unsatisfactory. That there should be anything unsatisfactory about the matter may be due to want of care on the part of the chief clerk in arranging the rate, or in issuing instructions to his assistants. It is most frequently due to carelessness or want of method in the assistants. In any case it may lead to confusion among the stations, and to infinite trouble with the traders. In this matter of rates the goods manager must depend upon the head of the department, who should know the line and its connections, and have some knowledge of its general traffic. This departmental head should also be conversant with the classification of goods—a kind of information supplied in a handy form by the Clearing House. Furnished with such important data as this, together with that familiarity with the company's special powers to which we have referred, he is in a position to quote new rates where traffic is being developed, or to modify old where these have proved prohibitory, and he will, wisely, be allowed a large discretion in this, so far as purely local traffic is concerned, and often in the case of foreign traffic also if he is judged to be capable. Where two or more companies are concerned in the quotation of a new, or in the alteration of an old rate, it will be his duty to correspond with the interested companies for their sanction. If these companies and the special traffic are amenable to Clearing House rule, and the rate is to be recorded on the Clearing House minutes, it will be necessary for the company proposing the change to report the agreement between the engaging companies to the Clearing House for record. If, however, the traffic is local to a company, but that company's neighbours have a right to acquiesce or object to an alteration as being competitors for the traffic, the company proposing the change need only receive the sanction of those companies to the adoption of the change. If the man in charge of such negotiations is of the right fibre, he may, as we have said, be safely left to carry out these arrangements without reference to the manager. Of course there are constantly arising great crucial questions between competitive companies, involving much more than the single quotation upon which such issues are raised. Then the manager conducts the discussion at the Managers' Conference as council, his rates clerk attending as agent, and advising. In all cases the manager attends the quarterly meetings at the Clearing House, when he can, in person; sometimes he is prompted and assisted by his lieutenant, the rates clerk, and sometimes that invaluable assistant attends for him. When a rate is arranged, the first duty is to engross it in the goods manager's book, and, from that, to issue it to all stations concerned. That duty must be left to junior assistants, and, as we have said, it is most important that none but careful lads should be entrusted with it. The amount of correspondence involved in the arrangement of rates is enormous, and, although it is often of a formal and stereotyped character, its very voluminousness must tax the energy and capacity of all concerned. There is not merely the quantity of penmanship to be got through; there is, previously, for the information of the clerk in charge, a certain amount of information to be collected from the books as to existing rates, for that or some similar class of goods, or for that of some adjacent place, with consultation as to the proper group of stations, with which the stations in question should be classed. All this occupies time, and it is no uncommon occurrence that men and lads, who have been straining every nerve to keep pace with the hours during the day, should, by force of such pressure of enquiry and investigation into a basketful of cases, be compelled to work late at night—nearly every night—to overtake the comparatively manual labour of writing the letters involved! Moreover, who is unfamiliar with the well-worn despatch-bag which the chief clerk of the rates department carries home full of papers which he has had no leisure to digest during the day, and brings back with him in the morning, the papers all dog-eared, with shorthand jottings for his assistants? But for shorthand, it would be impossible now-a-days to get through the mass of correspondence. By its means the goods manager dictates, and, almost immediately, signs the most important letters; and the hard-working and almost overpowered heads of departments indicate in a few slight strokes of the pencil, for one and another of the staff, the gist of the reply each may make, after his own manner, to this and that letter from the pile.

In the question of the value of shorthand in saving time where that is so precious, the department of "general correspondence" may be readily understood to be equally interested. Here, also, the head is the almost hourly recipient of such heaps of letters, reports, &c., upon such a variety of subjects as the uninitiated have no conception of—claims, complaints, reports, and returns, of so heterogeneous a character as, if catalogued, would weary the reader. Among these the claims bulk most largely in quantity, and demand a single word of notice. They are made for loss, or damage, or delay, and are founded on any or every pretext. The sender makes claim, or the receiver makes it. The claims clerk often having a separate responsibility from that of the "general" department, has a staff of his own. He has to get at the particulars of entry and the stations' report of affairs. This his assistants do. If the damage is clearly traceable to *his* company the claim has to be admitted, and the only question is then the fair amount chargeable. If it is not so clearly traceable to his company, the claims clerk reports the claim to the connecting companies in the linked transit of the goods, and thereafter ensues a correspondence, which occupies time and delays settlement, to the disappointment and impatience of the claimant, who, not understanding the causes of delay, and declaring he has nothing to do with the dispute between the companies, not unfrequently drags the company nearest him into court and gains his case. Then comes an appeal to the "Claims Arbitration Committee" of the Clearing House, which is prepared by the company compelled to pay, and, as we have said, that committee's decision is final. The claims clerk has usually a staff of inspectors of goods damaged in transit, who, in time, come to be very fair assessors of values, and are a most invaluable adjunct of this arm of the goods manager's corps. The head of the "general correspondence" department has supervision of stations, in their accounting, so far as goods traffic is concerned, and in the carrying out of instructions as to special traffic agreements and arrangements. He is expected to arrange the changes of goods train runnings, to have charge of goods guards and inspectors, to look to the working of the goods trains, the causes of decrease of traffic, if any, to receive canvassers' reports, and prepare the results for the goods manager's consideration, to keep the staff book, and to check the pay-bills; and, generally, to look after everything which affects the working of the goods traffic. Not unfrequently, in the case of companies having very wide districts, with divided management or superintendence, there is a periodical meeting of district goods managers or superintendents, and the head of the "general" department is often the clerk of the periodical conferences, calling the meetings, and keeping minutes of the proceedings. The work which he has to perform is multifarious and onerous, and he and his staff must be intelligent, energetic, and efficient.

In such a department as that of the goods manager, with so much responsibility and such various duty, a splendid field is open, and a young man entering upon such service has an honourable, if not learned, profession before him, the rewards of which are as fair as in any walk in life.

CHAPTER V.

THE GENERAL SUPERINTENDENT'S DEPARTMENT.

THE office of *general superintendent*, or *superintendent of the line* as it is variously styled, is one of the most responsible in the gift of a board of directors. He has the most expensive plant under his charge, and the lives of the travelling public in his control. Even when surrounded by highly competent assistants, a conscientious man in administering that high office must feel an ever-present dread of possible catastrophe from a thousand and one causes. It may seem a simple matter to the man who looks at a time-table that, even in the case of the most complicated systems, those who have been trained to the work should be able to construct one, and so, no doubt, it is; but when that has been most carefully arranged and due margin has been left for contingency, active though not nominal responsibility passes from the officers to the working staff — stationmasters, conductors, guards, engine-drivers, stokers, pointsmen, signalmen, crossing-keepers, goods and mineral drivers, and brakesmen, workmen in charge of the permanent way— everyone of these has the power of stultifying the most perfect arrangements for working over the line, and rendering them abortive, if not disastrous. Shakspeare represents Henry IV. as exclaiming in his distress, " Uneasy lies the head that wears a crown." There are few of our *general superintendents* who are free from a similiar uneasiness, though the crown they wear be but the bays they earn for their capacity. How many of them can leave the cares of office locked up in their bureaux when they retire to the quiet of their firesides, and the merry prattle of their children's voices? Does not every ring of the door-bell suggest possible calamity, and a call to scenes of dire disaster? Who among them can avoid the thought, as he lies down to well-earned sleep, that the midnight mail train, whose progress from point to point has been so carefully calculated, or the express goods train, whose shunts to clear the line for its more rapid neighbour have been arranged so accurately, may not *to-night*, from some slight overlook, one thoughtless act, one moment's want of watchfulness, plunge unsuspecting souls into instant and irrevocable death? This dreadful thought, we say, *must* sometimes visit the most able and conscientious of our superintendents; and, visiting them amid the happy influences of home, will doubtless imbue them with a finer sensibility to the dangers to which the splendid fellows who plunge through midnight darkness, flashing past myriad unseen risks, on engine foot-plates, or in luggage-piled brake-vans, are subject, and will help to produce that fine *esprit de corps* between officer and servant which should always subsist in the service, and by means of which the best work will certainly be done.

The *general superintendent* is responsible, as we have said, for the safe conduct of all traffic on the line. He drafts the time table—goods and mineral trains being arranged subject to his approval; he compiles the book of "rules and regulations" for the working of the traffic; has the charge of, and supreme control over stationmasters, porters, pointsmen, signalmen, crossing-keepers, and guards, and, with the exception of a very few of the higher class of stationmasters, he has, most generally, the appointment of the whole staff of his department. On some of the more important lines he has district officers with delegated powers, and is then relieved of much of the detail of the work; but on all lines he is the undisputed chief administrator over the line staff. To his office everybody reports upon everything. He must be fully informed of all that transpires in working the line. Guards send in their train journals, stationmasters their complaints, and their reports upon casualties of all kinds, and upon claims made for detention or loss, together with suggestions as to train arrangements, increase of accommodation, &c. Inspectors report the result of investigation into the complaints we have just referred to, of their inspection of signal boxes, and the working of signals, points, &c.; of the working of trains, and especially of the manipulation of excursion and other extraordinary traffic. The company's police apprise him of their movements for the detection and punishment of offenders against the letter of the eighth commandment and of the company's byelaws. The audit office advises of all cases of incapacity or carelessness in the keeping of station accounts, or the result of special investigation, where fraud or default is suspected or discovered. The telegraph brings the first faint echo of breakdown, collision, or other obstruction of the

line, and the post or next mail train bears confirmation, and gives form
and substance to the report by fulness of detail. The uninitiated can form
no fair conception of the *quantity* of sheets of writing paper, foolscap,
tea paper—the latter used by guards in writing up their train journals,
and by inspectors, pointsmen, signalmen, and often stationmasters—all
this necessary reporting to the superintendent's office implies, or, of its
bulk, when it all lies open upon his assistant's desk for distribution,
morning, noon, and rosy afternoon, as it comes in by every train. Its
bulk, and often its greatest troublesomeness, is mightily increased by the
necessary correspondence with other companies. Indeed, so great is the
volume of this delivery of paper, all day and every day, at the Superintendent's office, that it almost invariably falls to the duty of one member
of the staff to divide it among the departments as it comes in, each
department having a distinctive mark as a reference. While routine is
carried forward in the departments without reference to the superintendent direct, there are always a great many subjects with which the
superintendent alone can deal. In the course of the day, therefore, apart
from the necessary consultation with general manager, goods manager,
locomotive superintendent, engineer, secretary, or solicitor, the general
superintendent has frequently more than enough to occupy him in dealing
with specially knotty questions. He can usually keep a confidential shorthand clerk writing constantly to dictation; his grasp of subjects, each of
which is diverse, being, in the case of really capable men, perfected by the
habit of concentration of thought and attention upon what is *immediately
present*. If he travels he cannot leave this ever-pressing correspondence
behind him, or his deputy, with limited authority, is in difficulty as to
what to do with it. He therefore often carries his shorthand clerk and
his papers and note-books with him on his journeys, and, while fellow-
travellers are conning the day's news, skimming the latest novel, or
comfortably napping in a corner, this busy officer is reading, and pondering,
and dictating, while the clerk is practising the difficult art of writing
legible shorthand in an express train at full speed. So thoroughly
hemmed in is the superintendent with walls of reports and endless correspondence, and so constantly interrupted when busiest by an inquiring
public, that we can scarcely wonder if he seeks his holiday recreation—
short-lived and unfrequent as it too often is—among Scottish, Irish, or
Welsh mountain solitudes, where post, carrier, newsman, and telegraph
boy are alike unknown.

The general superintendent must be often from home visiting his stations. Notwithstanding his staff of intelligent and active inspectors, ever at his disposal to get at the whole facts of a difficult case, and the fulness of detail of reports prepared for him, a conscientious and energetic superintendent will feel the moral advantage of station visiting. He will feel that if this duty is performed in a kindly spirit his visits will be regarded as complimentary to the stationmaster's skill in management, or his care and orderliness in his arrangements. If station discipline is harsh, he hears of it, and can reduce chaotic elements to at least comparative harmony. If discipline is loose, he cannot fail to see it, and his periodical or incidental visits will prove to be beneficial checks. An observant officer will always travel with his eyes and ears open, and will often learn more in the course of a single glance along a platform while his train halts, or in a casual remark among fellow-passengers, of the character of the service given to the public, than he could ever hope to glean from reams of correspondence. By the exercise of this same faculty of observation he will also satisfy himself as to whether due prominence, in the most accessible places, is given to the company's time bills, and whether the *latest* are duly posted. He will often find it necessary to make incidental halts at stations for personal investigation of causes of complaint—the public *versus* the stationmaster, or the stationmaster *versus* some member of his staff—in cases where the statements made in writing to the office are conflicting. In addition to these he always holds a court of inquiry on the spot into the causes of accidents or casualties. These inquiries are usually made with the assistance and co-operation of the locomotive superintendent, and the permanent way engineer, and in certain cases the goods manager and mineral superintendent lend the aid of their counsels. The results of such inquiries are usually reported to the general manager, and are private and confidential. There is besides, however, a class of accidents into which the Board of Trade order investigation, and their inspector is sent down for that purpose. The superintendent has, on such occasions, to accompany the inspector to the scene, and to produce all who were in any way concerned in the accident, or who can throw any clear light upon its causes.

Subject to the approval of the general manager, the superintendent arranges all train runnings, both as to speed and stoppage, their working from main to branch lines, and *vice versa*, the goods manager conferring with and advising him as to goods and mineral train changes. He compiles the time tables and posters, and has charge of their distribution among the staff and the companies, and where through booking and continuous train-working with competitors, or more friendly companies, exists, he must consider and consult these before fixing hours of arrival or departure. He has, further, the arrangement of rates and fares, precisely the same rules guiding him to which we made reference in treating of the goods manager. For purely *local* traffic his company's special Acts alone limit his powers; but, wherever other companies are interested, they have to be consulted, and the Clearing House sanction to be obtained. On some of the more extensive systems there is, as we have already said, an officer, comparatively independent, to whom the distribution of carriage plant is entrusted; but the duty is frequently left to the superintendent. Where the latter is the practice the work he has to oversee is greatly increased.

The general superintendent is a member of the superintendents' conference which sits periodically in the Clearing House, in London or Dublin, as the case may be. He has his company's vote on all questions under discussion. As a rule he goes up to these conferences unattended; but, in his absence, he is represented by an assistant, usually his chief rates and fares clerk. When questions of detail on a large scale arise, such as the alteration of groups of stations, there is generally a meeting of these chief rates clerks summoned for the Clearing House Rooms, or some other convenient centre, and the details fully and freely discussed and minuted for the next superintendents' conference, where further discussion ensues and a decision is taken. At the conference meetings the superintendent exercises his sole legislative function.

This is, mayhap, a rapid and incomplete sketch of the general superintendent; but who shall peruse it and ponder the variety of the work he has to superintend, and its engrossing responsibility, and not feel that the office cannot be held efficiently by a man without wit and culture, who is also accustomed to be firm, with sauvity? The control of such an army, with its linked inter-dependence, implies the need of much and competent assistance. Accordingly a general superintendent's office will be found to embrace, as a rule, a duly qualified deputy, and such a variety of departmental clerks as there are important functions to be performed by the chief. And, firstly, let us glance at the office of deputy—he is often only chief clerk. Being in charge of an office into which reports and correspondence pour incessantly, he must be a man of energy, physical and mental, ready in resource, quick to apprehend, with force of character to enable him to decide promptly, and that ripe information which is needed to prevent that "repentance at leisure" which sometimes follows hasty decision. He is the administrator in the office, and must be apt in his administration—like his chief, gaining respect for his exercise of authority by its simple justice and its manifest humanity. He will often require to decide upon questions outside the office, to arbitrate in difficulties along the line, and that upon written information. He has reputation at stake in these cases also, and a good and true man will seek to do his duty in that on the strictest principles of justice without fear or favouritism. There is a high function to be fulfilled by all in authority, in this respect, which lies at the very root of all wholesome management. The stern rebuke of a really just and humane man tells with infinite force on *all* dispositions. The deputy must be a skilful disciplinarian, with this in view, for he has a large staff under his control, and efficient service will be won or lost according as he has tact, or wants it. He must be conversant with all the details of office work to be able to advise and instruct. Next to these high qualifications, he ought to be fairly cultured, and possessed of some native parts; as he should give tone and style to the correspondence issuing from the office, sending back for correction or re-writing, whatever is offensive to good taste. It may be urged that in a correspondence so voluminous it is idle to look for the graces of style and the higher courtesies; but we maintain that to the cultured it is as easy to be gracious as to the uncultured it is to be boorish; and we are desirous of holding up this view to the rising generation all the more that this is an age of cheap and effective intellectual drill. If the deputy is a man of the right stamp, he will know how to meet the public when they come with complaints, or to make inquiry. Some knowledge of what is needed in the construction of time-tables, and the arrangement of special trains, is indispensable, and also an acquaintance with the principles on which rates and fares are calculated. He should also keep a look-out upon the department having oversight of the running of trains, so that he may direct attention to the improvement of some, and suggest the discontinuance of others. His capacity as deputy will be best illustrated in relieving his chief of all matters with which he can honestly and rightly deal, and in drawing up sufficiently succinct *precis* of everything upon which the superintendent's opinion and instructions may be necessary to be taken. It should be his province so to manage that the superintendent shall have time to devote to the more active duties of his office; and, if he is a really competent lieutenant, he should have plenary powers. The chief rates clerk, for the due discharge of *his* office, should be well read in the geography of the railway system, and have an accurate knowledge of his company's powers, and of the Clearing House rules. He will be supplied with the Clearing House minutes from time to time, the details of which it will be his business to master, while he will find it advantageous to inform himself of the terms of agreement between his company and its competing neighbours. His books should always be kept so closely up, by the careful and prompt posting up of changes, that "he may read who runs." Indeed, in all railway offices no rule is more wholesome than this. The claims clerk should be chosen for a judicial quality of mind, not one who would too readily yield and pay, but one who, seeing that difficulties increase, by preventible delay, should have prescience to yield ere it be too late to effect compromise. The work in this department is not surrounded with such difficulties as in the goods department. It is, however, sufficiently onerous to call for skilful manipulation. The most serious of all claims in the passenger superintendent's hands are those made for compensation for personal injury. The time table department is a most important division of the superintendent's office work. The superintendent or his deputy indicates that certain trains are to come off or to be put on. Trains go in pairs, one up and one down, each corresponding with the other. If an up train is discovered to be running unremuneratively, it cannot be interfered with unless a down train can be dispensed with also, as the engines and carriages must *return*. It is accordingly no easy task so to arrange that the maximum of work may be got out of the engine and carriages with the minimum of working expense. That, however, must enter into the calculation of the superintendent and of his time table clerk. When the weather or time of year are not offering inducements to travellers, traffic by passenger trains is light. These purely temporary incidents cannot, however, be allowed to affect the efficiency of a good staff of guards, whose services will soon again be in full requisition. So, when trains are discontinued for a time, these men are drafted off to some other duty, to be ready, at call, to assume their old places. In the matter of merely changing the times of departure and arrival of trains the superintendent simply indicates the leading times, and leaves the passing and stopping times to be calculated by the time-table clerk. The duty of finishing and printing these fresh monthly or incidental time tables is very onerous, the safety of the line being dependent upon their accuracy. The severest critics of the time tables are the drivers and guards—whose experience of running is so thoroughly practical. If the alteration ordered or contemplated meets with their approval it may be said that its success is ensured. The time table department has also the preparation of time tables for all special traffic, special goods, mineral, and passenger trains, and in the case of all such, separate slips have to be issued "to all concerned." When the line is under repair at any point, and single line has to be worked, special slip notices are printed and distributed to all engaged in working traffic over the section, informing them of the special regulations. made. The issue of time tables and posters is a very important matter, and involves much experience, tact, and care. The chief companies, besides serving copies upon every man concerned—even the platelayers requiring to be supplied —are in the habit of sending them out to all hotels in the country, to steamship proprietors, and also to each other. The chief clerk of such a department must, therefore, be a painstaking, careful man—methodical in habit—and his assistants equally so. The men upon whom devolves the work of examining the train journals as they are delivered—and guards and brakesmen are expected to make these out and deliver them as soon after they reach the end of each double journey as possible—must also be careful and smart. The chief object of examining these is to ascertain whether trains are keeping time, and the causes of obstruction, and to endeavour to arrange for improved working. These are the principal departments into which the superintendent's staff is divided. The main body of the clerks must be accurate, swift, and neat penmen. They should be fairly educated; the higher and broader and more liberal their education, the better fitted are they for promotion, and the more useful in their several spheres. A knowledge of shorthand is now almost indispensable in the office of the superintendent, and, as we have said, it is easily acquired, where it is unknown. No novice is now engaged, who is not in some degree familiar with its signs.

CHAPTER VI.

THE DEPARTMENT OF PERMANENT WAY AND WORKS.

THE engineer is the head of this most invaluable scientific, designing branch of railway service. He is charged with the construction and maintenance of the line and all relative works, and is responsible for the safe condition of bridges and station premises, and also for the smooth working of points and signals. If he is active and conscientious, it is not difficult to perceive that he is a busy man, and that official cares must frequently press heavily, following him home and disturbing his rest. This we have had occasion to say of other officers; and we may say here, that all railway officers engaged in working the traffic over the line, or in keeping that line in good working order, are more or less subject to anxiety, by night even more than by day, lest something should go wrong. The engineer is, as we have said, no exception to this rule, as, even when his personal supervision is close and constant, unexpected flood may imperil, if it does not carry away, a bridge here, or wash away an embankment there. In times of frost rails are in danger of fracture. Sudden thaw after severe snow and ice endangers embankments on the sides of mountain ranges by splitting boulders on the heights and precipitating huge masses of rock on the line, or it cracks the rocky walls of deep cuttings and renders the passage of heavy trains at high speed perilous. Heavy rains overload sand and clay embankments, and they slip and block the line. Snow drifts in open moorland or mountainous districts have the same effect. The inner walls and roofs of tunnels, whether built or formed of the natural rock, from the same or relative causes give way, often without warning, and not only impede traffic but render travelling unsafe. These and a thousand-and-one minor accidents, only looked for in a general way, and all possible, as we have said, under the most careful supervision, are cause of special anxiety to the engineer, and he is happily constituted if he can maintain an ordinarily cheerful disposition and divest himself of bogus terrors, possessing his soul in calmness till the hour of trial arrives.

On all railway systems the initial duty of the engineer is to make survey of the ground over which a line is proposed to be laid; to advise the promoters as to cost, and as to the cheapest, because the most serviceable route for catching traffic, looking also to ease of construction; to prepare plans and sections, with maps for Parliamentary warfare; and to be in his place, as a principal witness, before Parliament, when the Bill becomes before that tribunal—all this he does in concert with the company's solicitor, and, in the later stages, with their Parliamentary agent. In the earlier stages the utmost care is required lest the "standing orders" should be in the smallest detail neglected. The Parliamentary plans and sections must be prepared with the greatest accuracy in detail, and this often in the face of much opposition when the landowners or farmers are hostile to the scheme. All the preliminary field work has to be done at the risk of being treated as a trespasser or worse, and many good stories are told of the expedients which have to be resorted to for outwitting irate agriculturists. Carelessness in the initiatory stages is certain to prove fatal to the project, and to the engineer's opportunity of proving his quality as a witness, because the Bill runs the risk of being rejected by the examiner. If he is lucky enough to have performed his work carefully, his plans and sections precede him to the committee room, where he meets them in enlarged form on the walls, and he passes examination and then cross-examination on them. Here he is happy if he escapes without loss of temper, since he is certain to be assailed from all points by counsel anxious to make good the opposition views of their clients, and their reputation as sharp fellows. Some of our engineers are witnesses of the first water. Full of their case, they offer nothing that is not wanted, and sometimes baffle the chaffing counsel on the other side by their coolness, firmness, and self-possession. The Bill having been obtained, the engineer's next duty is to draw out detailed specifications, with working plans, for the contractors who may be selected for the construction of the line. It is matter of considerable satisfaction to the companies, and cause of just pride on the part of our engineers, that so little discrepancy occurs, as a rule, between the estimated and the actual cost of making our lines, and it proves the care and the technical skill of these officers that results so nearly accurate can be arrived at, as it were, hypothetically. Parliamentary committees are not prone to pass the preambles of bills for the construction of *expensive* works, so that there is a tendency on the part of promoters to prove that their lines are to be constructed for a mere bagatelle, and their engineers are, therefore, prompted to prove this by a process not unlike that of *undervaluing*. That it should, under such a system, therefore, so seldom be necessary to apply for further money powers in subsequent sessions, is, as we have said, in the highest degree creditable to our engineers.

The " Act " being passed, the engineer has to set out the line on the ground, and as he is now no longer subject to be treated as a wandering vagabond, being protected by statute, which imposes heavy penalties on any one molesting him, or interfering with his work, he has the opportunity of making a more careful study of the route, and of adopting such modifications, within certain limits, on his original line and levels as he may deem advisable. In preparing plans for the works, the engineer has among other things to design station premises at roadsides and at termini. Those at the latter in the nature of things require more expensive treatment than roadside stations, so that our officer, skilled in lineal and cubic measurement, must develop equal knowledge of, and skill in the art and science of architecture. He has to prepare working plans of the whole works, to design the bridges—stone and ironwork—to consider the strain the latter may be required to bear, and to make provision; to specify the quantity of excavation needful, to indicate, where he can, whether that be of rock or earth, also the quantity of earth required for filling up, where low ground has to be embanked; to indicate the weights, and give sections of the rails to be used, and to work out the plans of all crossings, and through shunts; to lay out all mineral and goods yards, and to arrange the working of points and signals—all this, and probably much more which we may have overlooked, the engineer has to do, preparatory to the issue of advertisements for " tenders " for the works. When these latter are received and opened they are handed to the engineer for his report upon them, and the directors or promoters usually act upon his advice, and accept the offer which he recommends. The contract for works having been adjusted and signed, and the work of construction begun, the engineer and his assistants become inspectors for the nonce, taking oversight of the work at various points in order to its being faithfully performed, and also in order that they may be able to certify for the contractor's periodical payments. All ironwork, girders, pillars, brackets, rails, upon which there is likely to be *strain*, is carefully inspected while under construction, and is tested by the engineer's staff before being accepted, so that the risk of slop work, where so much life and property are at stake, is reduced to its minimum. When the whole works are completed, and the government inspection passed, a process, by the way, not so easy as might be expected, after such care in planning and constructing, but one in which the officer appointed by the Board of Trade has to satisfy himself that the construction is sound, in theory and in fact, that signals are properly seen at certain distances, and that travelling on the line is theoretically safe, the company receives from the Board of Trade a formal sanction to open the line. For twelvemonths after the completion of the works it is the duty of the contractor, under stipulation of most deeds of contract, to maintain the works. After the expiry of that period, their care and up-keep, hitherto a *capital* charge, being now transferred to the company and the company's engineer, or permanent way and works department, become chargeable upon *revenue*. The works being completed, the duty of measuring the work done, and of adjusting the accounts with the various contractors, devolves upon the engineer. On extensive works this is a very tedious matter, involving the examination of all details where there have been alterations on the work from that shown on the contract drawings and described in the specification. It is usual to make provision in the contract for any difference arising in these matters to be settled by arbitration, and it says much for the fairness, tact, and capacity of our engineers that resort to an arbitration is of comparatively rare occurrence.

When the line has been opened, and traffic is yielding revenue, and in its passage is finding out the weak places in the materials or faults in construction, or is *developing* beyond expectation, the engineer and his staff are, as we stated in the beginning, fully employed with sufficiently engrossing and anxious work. Conditions of the weather affect some of the materials. Some portions of the line are more liable than others to get out of order, either by reason of there being a greater rush of traffic between certain points, or because of something faulty in the nature of the ground over or through which those portions have been laid, or, as in the case of tunnels, the roofs, walls, rails, and sleepers are subject to constant deterioration by water dripping or oozing through.

Charged with such duties, and laden with so many and grave responsibilities, it seems needful that the engineer should be a man fertile of resource. To this end he must be master of the *theory* of his profession, and have a thorough experience of its *practice*. In a great engineer these are as inseparable as the Siamese twins. Theoretically, he may be able to calculate strains and deflections to a demonstration, but that which looks well on paper does not always, or necessarily, turn out well in working. It will therefore be manifest that an engineer, to be successful, should be master also of the practical part of his profession. He must know enough of the manufacture of ironwork of all kinds needful to the construction and repair or replacement of works, to enable him to judge of its fitness for its purpose. He must have sufficient experience of mason and joiner work to check the use of insufficient materials, or the employment of fair materials in a way not provided for in the specification. If he is not an architect he must employ one to design stations and offices; and it needs no demonstration to prove the great value of an accurate and scientific knowledge of that branch of his profession to an engineer. The man who possesses it is much more likely to do satisfactory work than he who has to delegate it to a specialist, and he will do it with greater pleasure to himself. The employment of an architect implies many consultations with one who has no technical or special acquaintance with railway requirements, and consequently cannot design so accurately; and it also supposes possible conflict of opinion, and therefore delay and worry. Most of our handsome station premises in the country are the work of our engineers, and, in their taste and completeness, are a memorial of their capacity. In the work of laying out new lines, an engineer who is a geologist will derive much practical aid from that science. He will know something of the sub-superficial condition of the country through which his line is projected. The solid contents of its mountain ranges will be comparatively familiar, and the causes and character of the undulations on its valleys will be an open book to him. From this scientific standpoint he will be able to avoid projecting his line through ground which would require hard or heavy excavation, and where that is unavoidable he will be better able to estimate the cost of excavation through rock or clay, the character of which he is in a position to describe without the expense of boring. Geology is of still greater use to the engineer in spanning rivers and arms of the sea, as, the character, the depth, and dip of the sub-aqueous bed being to a certain extent familiar to him, he can the more readily ascertain and gauge the difficulties to be encountered in sinking his piers. We do not say it is *necessary* he should be a geologist, we simply affirm that he who *is* one, is a much more valuable engineer—other things being equal, of course—than the man who is not. The broader the culture, as we have remarked, the greater the chance of success, the greater the independence, and the higher the authority. The engineering mind is essentially scientific, so that *all* science, especially such as has any bearing upon his profession, must be attractive; and it would be more wonderful to find him negligent than well furnished in that direction.

In describing the engineer, we are to be understood as including the district engineers of the more extensive systems, and the principal assistants. The same high and broad capacities must be there in full operation, or only waiting opportunity for display. Otherwise the enormous and onerous work of the department could never be overtaken. In their districts the district officers conduct all operations which do not materially affect the dividend-paying capacity of the line, such as repairs, slight alterations, and general maintenance. Where there are district engineers, the chief engineer acts as a consulting officer, whose head and hands are free from the worry of petty details of ordinary maintenance. Where there is no such sub-division of responsibility, the principal assistant takes charge of all but the greater questions of extension, remodelling, &c. He superintends the whole staff, both of assistants and of workmen out of doors. He trains the apprentices, distributes the work to draughtsmen, inspectors, &c., and supervises the technical work of the office generally. There is one qualification in which he should excel. He should be a correct and ready draughtsman. His influence over the staff in the office will be greatly increased if he possesses this undoubtedly useful accomplishment in common with those others to which we referred in describing the engineer. He should also be a wise and prudent administrator, capable of selecting the best men for every class of duty, and of commanding their esteem. It is from the ranks of these junior officers that the engineers who initiated the railway system, and are dropping out of the muster-roll, are from time to time replaced. *That* is their incentive to hearty work. Equally, it is from the ranks of the junior assistants, usually all qualified engineers, and the apprentices, as the latter complete their course of studies and their period of active service, that the principal assistants' successors are draughted, and *that* is *their* expectation, if, indeed, by great diligence and application, they do not hope to reach the highest place. The work of the engineer's office demands a variety of accomplishments in the members of the staff. They must be *students*, but they must not grudge to be workmen also. They have to undergo fatiguing work in the fields, surveying and levelling in all weathers. They must be able to sustain vigorous life, ever and anon, as occasion requires, on such food as moor and moss and mountain-side offer, and they require to bend themselves nearly double over their drawing boards, straining their eyes over the drawing of plans with lines of most trying compactness, or they have occasion to go on hands and knees on the floor over drawings on a larger scale, till knees and back and eyes are fain to complain. Many of these fine fellows are to be found at the arduous field or office practice of their profession during long terms, and yet find time and brain for study of its science, its hard-headed theory. These are the men who cleave their way to eminence. The laggards rarely rise above the level of scarcely very reliable draughtsmen. Mathematics, engineering, and drawing are among the essential studies of an apprentice who would excel, and these may be conducted either simultaneously with the practical office and field work or, better still, when it can be done, before entering upon the practical.

The department requires a staff of clerks and book-keepers for necessary correspondence and the due care of the expenditure. This portion of the staff is presided over by a principal commercial assistant.

CHAPTER VII.

THE TELEGRAPH ENGINEER.

WHAT the railway system would be without the powerful aid of electricity, it is difficult to realise at present. Familiarity with the combination produces in the minds of all a spirit of happy carelessness of the condition of things prior to the introduction of the science of telegraphy. Even those who can recollect its introduction rarely consider under what serious disadvantages railways were worked in the old days, while the younger railway men—always excepting the thoughtful and curious—accustomed to its aid accept that aid as a matter of course, and think nothing about the "old time before them." Of course when railways were in their infancy, trains were fewer, with lower rates of speed. As that great enterprise took a firmer hold on popular favour it shot out arms everywhere. New and competing lines were constructed. Near the great manufacturing and commercial centres, intersection on the level began to be introduced. Greater distances were run over by-and-bye; competition begat speed, and this again, with the growth of innumerable intersections, created danger, or delays hitherto not experienced. It was then that the electric telegraph came to the front and developed its marvellous resources. To quote from a most interesting and instructive paper on "Telegraphy: Its Rise and Progress in England," by William Henry Preece, C.E. and T.E., Divisional Engineer, Postal Telegraph Department, a paper read at the Royal Albert Hall, London, on July 18th, 1872:—" Prior to 1837," he says, "the telegraph instrument was but a scientific toy. The first practical form of instrument in England was invented by Messrs. Cooke and Wheatstone. On the 25th July of that year, a trial was made from Euston to Camden Town, through wires $1\frac{1}{4}$ miles in length, placed underground. It was tried on the Great Western Railway from Paddington to West Drayton in 1838. Mr. G. P. Bidder introduced it practically on the

Blackwall Railways in 1840, in working the rope system on that line; and in 1841, Mr. Locke ordered a short line from the Queen Street Station, at Glasgow, to Cowlairs. In 1842-3 the Great Western telegraph was continued from West Drayton to Slough, to illustrate a new and cheap method of suspending wires in the air. The first form was called the 'Hatchment' telegraph, from its resemblance to those strange objects on the fronts of our mansions which provincials gaze at with so much wonder. Many will remember the intense excitement produced on the public mind by the apprehension of Tawell, the murderer, by means of this very telegraph. A young woman had been murdered on January 1st, 1845. The following message was sent from Slough:—'A murder has just been committed at Salthill, and the suspected murderer was seen to take a first-class ticket for London, by the train which left Slough at 7.42 p.m. He is in the garb of a Quaker, with a brown greatcoat on, which reaches nearly down to his feet; he is in the last compartment of the second first-class carriage.'"

Tawell was apprehended, convicted, and executed. Few know how nearly the ends of justice were frustrated. The instrument makes no "Q" or "Z." The word "quaker" could only be spelt "KWAKER," and it was with the greatest difficulty that the orthography could be comprehended. The message had to be repeated several times, and in consequence it was considerably delayed.

In 1843 a short line was erected in Ireland (Mr. Preece does not say where), and another upon the Leeds and Manchester Railway in England; but in 1844, the first line of any length was constructed from London (Nine Elms) to Gosport, upon the London and South-Western Railway.

It was not till 1846, however, that it took root, and that a company was formed in England for its establishment as a commercial undertaking.

These extremely interesting historical facts we have thought well worthy of a place in this chapter, and we make no apology for inserting them. We must, however, offer Mr. Preece an expression of our great indebtedness to him for them.

Some eminent electricians, among them Sir Wm. Thomson, hold the opinion that electricity will be the motive power of the future. We have seen such marvels of science during the past fifty years, that to deny the possibility of this theory becoming fact is to repeat the incredulousness of our fathers at the inception of railways. We cannot limit the possibilities of science. We wait the development of research with a calm hopefulness that there are many things—many forces in Nature of which we wot not—only biding their time to yield their secrets to the earnest truth-seeker. Whatever electricity may yet do for man one thing is certain. It has already, in conjunction with the railway, advanced civilization, commerce, international community of interest and good feeling, and sweetened the cup of life, for all, incalculably. The telegraph wires—which are spread overhead in our large cities, and stretch from pole to pole along our highways, and on our railway banks, like æolian harps of giant dimensions—are constantly, during the night as well as in the busy day, charged with tidings of joy or of woe to myriads. They carry the message which summons the medical man to his patient's couch, or flash the news of his death to sorrowing relatives. By their agency the operator on stocks in the Exchange is advised of dividends on which he is speculating, and on which success or the reverse may be depending. So, also, is the merchant of modern times indebted to it for early news of the success of trading speculation abroad, or he may, by its aid, advise his foreign representatives when and what to sell, and at what price. Its extension by submarine cable across thousands of miles of ocean has been an incalculable boon to the merchant and manufacturer in the direction just indicated. And the development of the science of meteorology owes much to the telegraph cable, both aerially-stretched and submerged, for by its assistance those patient and indefatigable men of science, who are in charge of meteorological stations in this country and on the continent of America, have been able to decide to an almost certainty the laws of aerial currents, their rates of speed, and their force, and to predict the day, and almost the time of day on and at which a particular storm will reach our shores, and what special point it will attack. In this way the telegraph wire is an agent for good whom the sailor must recognise with intense delight. It puts up the *block-signal* against his leaving his station, and thus saves him the desperate chances of a collision with the elements. This reference to *block-signals* brings us back to the railway and the telegraph. Such wonderful immunity from serious accident as we enjoy—and undoubtedly there is great immunity, considering the hundreds of thousands who travel by rail daily—we owe to the telegraph system. Long distances are run by competing companies, often over intersecting lines, by day and by night at high express speed, and with such a sense of security, that passengers go to sleep, and sleep soundly, without even *thought* of risk. This would be impossible, as we have already hinted, but for the aid of the telegraph wire. At the suggestion of inspecting officers of the Board of Trade, who have been sent to investigate into the causes of accidents as they have occurred, the system of block-signalling and interlocking points has been very generally adopted. The block-signal is simply an application of telegraphy to railway train working by which the approach of every train is signalled from cabin to cabin along the route, each signalman being responsible for the safe passage of trains over his section of the line. Since the adoption of this system the number of serious accidents on our great trunk lines has very sensibly diminished.

In the year 1870 the State took over the telegraph property of the various commercial companies who had hitherto conducted the business of telegraphy. Under State management many changes were effected in the public interest, to which it is no part of our subject to do more than refer. The telegraph companies' interests in the wires stretched along the railway routes were, of course, bought up, and the State came in the place of these companies as tenants of the railway companies for " way leave." The companies have each special arrangements with the telegraph department of the Post-office for maintenance of the State wires, a duty which they perform in conjunction with the maintenance of their own. A company's wires are used for traffic purposes, and for speedy transmission of instructions, or of reports that will not wait the delay of writing in the first instance, such as accidents, requiring the aid of gangs of workmen, or the skilled advice of engineer or passenger superintendent.

The superintendent of a railway telegraph department has many and onerous duties to perform. He has charge of the erection, maintenance, and working of the whole telegraph system on his company's lines. These duties include, as we have already said, the erection and maintenance of all Government and private wires running upon his company's poles. The duties of his department may be classified under two heads—viz., the engineering and the commercial. Under the first are included the erection and maintenance of poles, wires, supports, instruments, batteries, cables, piping, boxing, leading-in, earth-wires, &c., necessary for keeping up speaking, block, and other telegraphs. He arranges for the fitting-up and erection of telegraphs upon new lines, and also arranges the necessary circuits and connections for the traffic requirements, and for extensions upon existing lines, as the working may necessitate from time to time.

When a new line is about to be opened the superintendent goes over the route, to make a careful survey, taking special notice of the nature of the ground, and the general exposure of the road, for the purpose of choosing the most suitable side for erecting the poles. This done, he walks over and measures the ground, marking out the place for each pole, choosing the most suitable points, conformable with regularity, so that each pole or support may be able to bear its share of the strain to be put upon it. He decides upon the number and varied heights of the poles, according to the number of wires each has to carry, and the peculiarities of the line, making the necessary allowance for additional height at level crossings, junctions, and bridges, and for guarding the wires at certain places, so that, in the event of a breakage, the road or rail may not be fouled. In this walk over the new route the telegraph superintendent marks out the positions of instruments and batteries at the various stations and cabins, and he arranges for leading-in and earth wires.

This being done, the requisite materials are calculated and provided for the work, and, in due course, forwarded to the nearest point on the scene of operations, and the erection proceeded with under the care of a qualified inspector. The ground, during the work of erection, is walked over by the superintendent from time to time as the work progresses, until completion. Then the wires are tested, and the speaking and block circuits are connected, each station on the older circuits being advised of his code, and supplied with a list of corresponding stations.

The extension of sidings, station yards, buildings, and cabins make continual claims upon the telegraph superintendent's attention—these extensions and alterations frequently entailing the removal of poles and wires out of the way of contractors' operations, as it is imperative that the wires be kept clear of the slightest contact with each other, or with the earth. This work, moreover, requires to be performed with the greatest caution, so that the continuity of a wire may not be interrupted in any way, and thereby cause a break in the communication.

Continual supervision, requiring the frequent walking of the lines, has to be exercised in the maintenance of poles, wires, insulators, &c., as even the breakage of one wire may interrupt a number of others, and thus seriously interfere with communication until repaired. Instruments require to be regularly tested and cleaned, and, when necessary, renewed.

The elements are always a source of anxiety to the superintendent, whether on duty or off, sudden frosts causing contraction and breakage; while heavy gales often play sad havoc, blowing down the poles, and breaking the wires; but the most dreaded storm is that of snow, followed by a gale, for while the wires are coated, and heavily weighed down with snow, and tossed to and fro by the ruthless wind—no matter how strong they may be—they are often unable to resist the weight and strain cast upon them, and are liable to be levelled to the ground. In such circumstances immediate repairs are absolutely necessary; neither wind nor weather are allowed to interfere. The work of repair must be performed in some way, and through communication restored as speedily as possible. For not only is railway traffic seriously interfered with the while, but the Government telegraphic or public wires are stopped. This latter is serious enough; but so also is the interruption of the company's telegraphic communication, for, as we have said, it is only since the use of the telegraph that it has been possible to keep up the multitudinous rush of trains in such constant succession, and at such rates of speed, with such wonderful immunity from accident.

The quality of wire insulators and materials generally requires to be carefully examined and tested before being sent out, in order to the greatest efficiency in working.

The superintendent generally has the assistance of capable inspectors, whose duty it is to take charge of certain lengths, these lengths, again, being divided into sections in charge of resident linemen at the most accessible stations. These linemen report to the superintendent daily, by wire, after ascertaining the condition of their circuits, letting him know where they are to be working for the day. Every fault on the Government system of wires is also reported by wire to the superintendent, so that he has the condition of the wires and apparatus of the whole system on his office table daily. Test boxes are placed at certain stations, so that a fault may be localised quickly within a given area.

At head-quarters there is usually a workshop, under the charge of a competent instrument maker, for the construction and repair of instruments, and for the making and renewal of batteries and other materials necessary for the upholding of the apparatus generally. The instruments now in use on the railway systems are exceedingly varied and complex, comprising speaking, block-instruments, repeators, bells, route indicators, train and dock indicators, and many other special appliances for particular work on various lines and branches.

Under what may be called the commercial department of the telegraph system is included the business of carrying telegrams for traffic requirements, which, on an extensive system of railways, requires considerable care and arrangement. Upon instruments devoted to signalling messages devolves much of the commercial correspondence of a railway staff, for, by the aid of these speaking instruments, irregularities are avoided, time is saved, and plant is moved about expeditiously and judiciously, the greatest amount of work taken out of it, and money is earned and saved. To effect this, however, a carefully-organised system of working the telegraph is required. A rule book is compiled from which every necessary instruction may be gleaned. By means of the telegraph "time" is circulated once a day over a whole railway system—stations and cabins alike. The superintendent arranges the circuits in the way best suited to the working, taking care to place the principal stations in direct communication with head-quarters. Central transmitting stations are arranged at convenient and busy points so as to circulate messages in the most expeditious manner. It can easily be imagined that on a railway extending over hundreds of miles a staff of clerks is absolutely necessary—good telegraph operators all—careful, steady and attentive. These clerks, men and women, are, of course, controlled from the centre of operations by the superintendent. At many stations the railway companies act as agents for the Postmaster-General in the collection and delivery of public telegrams, and in the transfer of these messages to and from the postal system. For this purpose handing-over circuits are connected between the local post-office and the railway at convenient points.

The telegraph superintendent is, it will be judged from all this, a hard-working railway officer. Like the passenger superintendent and the permanent way engineer he is apt to find that, no matter how fully occupied his day has been, his cares are certain, now and again, to find him out at home, and to drag him from the family circle. Whatever else may stand over till to-morrow, and whatever the condition of the weather, the telegraphic communication, on which everything that concerns the working of the line and the traffic depends, *must* be kept up, or restored where interrupted, and without loss of time. He is a great traveller. By rail when he can, but perhaps no other officer—excepting, perhaps, the permanent way engineer—*walks* the lines so frequently. He must, therefore, be a man of good physique. His primary professional qualification is, however, that he be an electrician. A thorough mastery of electricity—as applied to the telegraph—is a *sine qua non*. Without this scientific knowledge he could not arrange the strength of his batteries, could not charge them, repair his instruments, arrange his circuits, plant his signal cabins, decide as to the best means of insulating earth cables, or perform the thousand-and-one duties of supervision of the scientific part of his work of construction and repair. He is the fountain-head of advice in all emergencies—both scientific and mechanical. And this leads us to observe, further, that he is nothing if not also an engineer. He must possess sufficient mechanical skill to know how and where, most safely, to erect his poles, and to support them; what weight of wire each can carry; what strain the wires are likely to stand in stretching. And he must be able to judge of the value of the several wires in testing them, in order to economy and efficiency. Having many assistants, he does not necessarily perform much manual labour, either mechanical or scientific; but as we have said, he should possess sufficient knowledge and skill to be able to apply his hand to anything; and, therefore, in supervision of others, to be in a position to instruct as to the best methods. He will be surrounded by electricians and engineers, who will receive instruction and advice, and profit by example in following the daily round of their duties. His most efficient assistants will, like himself, be imbued with scientific enthusiasm—students of chemistry, who are never satisfied that they know enough in the domains of that most wonderful of the sciences. It will be a source of pleasure to him to help them in their eager pursuit of his own favourite study; and they in turn will render him earnest work and whole-hearted zeal. It is inconceivable that either he or they can be content to be men of one idea. Being practical scientists they are certain to reach forward into cognate science, and to broaden their vision by wide culture.

The telegraph operator is not necessarily a scientific man. His special duties, as operator, make no demand upon him but that of skill in manipulating his instrument, and a thorough grasp of his code of signs. He should never be satisfied to remain ignorant of the science which gives life and energy to the instruments he works, however, because he becomes by so much the more a valuable telegraphist, and, when least he thinks it, he may be observed, and bidden " go up higher." There is no altitude beyond the reach of the painstaking and persevering.

The superintendent's office-work is managed by a principal in-door assistant, and is carried on by a staff of clerks whose duties are, in the main, much like those of the other departments of railway work.

NOTE.—Since writing the foregoing we have been put in possession of this important fact, supplied by Mr. Edward Graves, Engineer of the Post-office Telegraphs, in his paper, " A Decade in the History of English Telegraphy," recently read before the Society of Telegraph Engineers in London :—" The apparatus used by the railway companies in the United Kingdom is nearly four times greater than that used by the Post-office, for while of message, block, and repeating-instruments the railway companies use 46,847, the Post Office only use 12,000."

CHAPTER VIII.

THE LOCOMOTIVE DEPARTMENT.

OUR progress through the various departments discloses for us the fact that each has its own intrinsic importance. Now and again we are tempted, as we contemplate the responsibilities which devolve upon the principal of the department then under consideration, to think that here at last we have come upon the most important, the most indispensable arm of the service. The ever-recurring thought, as fresh vistas of work with a wrinkle-making anxiety in it open up before us, alone saves us from the mistake that any department is intrinsically more honourable than the others. Each has its native cares, its special usefulness. All are essential and indispensable parts of one great whole; all are alike charged with the duty of looking to the general good, of working for the common interest. We have said that it is difficult to avoid unduly magnifying the relative importance of some of the departments in our survey of their individual work; but, on the whole, we feel that we are in a better position to estimate their intrinsic and relative advantages than the respective and respected heads, or the members of their staffs, for have they not a pardonable and natural tendency to-look at their own duties through a magnifying lens, and upon their neighbours' through the narrow end of a binocular. The excellence of any man's work depends upon the thorough practical knowledge of its details which he brings to bear upon it. This thoroughness cannot be acquired by the dilettanti. It is only likely to be his who confines himself to one pursuit, and tries to master it. This very absorption, this exclusiveness of aim, so essential to fitness for good work, is, however, as everyone knows, apt to lead us all to think *our own* occupation the most indispensable, *our own* work the first in rank and importance. This is a fair excuse for the partiality and self-complacency with which the capable members of a departmental staff view their own labour and estimate its value relatively to the whole; but, as we have stated, our survey of each with reference to that whole, should enable us more accurately to gauge the value and pretensions of rival claims to superiority, and to priority of place. It is, however, no part of our scheme to indicate distinctions such as these; it would not be to edification, and if it were, the general result of our survey has been to throw distinctions of so invidious a character into the shade, and to satisfy us that every department is essential, and, therefore, most important in its own place in the system.

The primary objects for which railways have been constructed are that the public and its merchandise may be served, and that profits may be made, out of which the promoters may have dividends. To these ends we must first have the engineer and his assistants to make the road; then we discover the need of carrying capacity, we require carriages, waggons, and engines, all which, as every railway *employé* knows, are technically designated the *rolling stock*. While the engineer is laying down the line, the company is busy building this *rolling stock*, or *plant*. This work is given out to various builders, by contract, with the stipulation that it shall all be ready for delivery by the time of opening the line for traffic. Before this important work is contracted for by the company requiring it, a most essential office has to be filled, that, namely, of the locomotive superintendent. That officer is appointed from among a host of capable, practical, and theoretical mechanical engineers. He must be able to design carriages, waggons, vans, engines, &c., as the work of building these will be certain to be entrusted to him.

Not that, in the case of a new company, he will construct the new plant in the company's workshops, but that he will make the drawings and specifications for the builders, and, when the contracts have been let, will see that they are fully, fairly, and efficiently fulfilled. None but a thorough theorist could design correctly, and with confidence of the result, while the mere theorist would fail in discovering what, to the practical man, would be patent, in mal-construction or defective workmanship. The most useful locomotive engineer, then, is he who has been thoroughly grounded in the theory and practice of his profession, who has passed through the workshops, learning the art and science of fitting and erecting, who can handle all necessary tools, work at the various machines, and make designs. He must have skill in drawing, taste and facility in design, and be a mathematician and algebraist, in order to be able to work out quantities accurately and rapidly, and to calculate strains. If during his graduation period he has used his eyes carefully, and made observation a branch of his study, he will have some useful knowledge of materials, and be able to test their quality and fitness for his purpose. In this way he will have acquired skill in selecting materials, so that, with a moderate degree of certainty, he may choose this and reject that from the mass. With the exception of mathematics and algebra, the locomotive engineer gains his knowledge in a practical way throughout the years of his apprenticeship, in his passage through the shops to the drawing office. The exceptional branches of study must be pursued in the usual way, by attendance at classes, and no efficient work can be done without close application. It has not unfrequently happened that much has been acquired by patient men with the genius of earnestness, in mastering the abstruse problems of the mathematician and algebraist, by self-culture; and we honour most highly the men who have conquered difficulties in that hard and thorny way. We set no limit to the breadth of culture, esteeming those most worthy of promotion, and most likely to illuminate the highest offices, who have used their leisure in enlarging their knowledge, if they are careful not to allow collateral reading to interfere with the most thorough equipment for their special duties. The wisest among ambitious men are they who confine the range of their studies to such as throw additional light upon their more immediate pursuits, and enable them to follow these with a higher intelligence. Among collateral studies in which a locomotive engineer would do well to embark, there is probably none so intrinsically and relatively interesting as that of chemistry. Apart from its special adaptability to the wants of his profession, that branch of science has attractions innumerable, and yields rewards to the patient and industrious which encourage him on the very threshold. Its advantages to the mechanical engineer are, however, very great. With a knowledge of its principles, he is in a position to test, with precision, the value of metals, both in respect of the price charged for them, and their suitableness for his purpose. He knows the proportions of the various alloys necessary, can speak to the qualities of the primary metals, such as tin and copper, and can tell whether iron and steel have been properly produced, and are likely to bear the theoretical strain.

These are at least some of the qualifications which the locomotive engineer acquires during his graduation period in the shops, the drawing office, the class-room, and the study. He has learned, besides, how to drive an engine, to work it smoothly and cautiously, to keep it in good working order, to repair trifling defects or damages by the way, and to overhaul it when in "stable;" while he is at home in more serious repair and reconstruction in the art of turning it out of the shops when it has become aged and worn, with new equipments and new vigour for a fresh lease of life. There is another qualification which the high office of locomotive superintendent demands, which is neither to be acquired in the shop nor the study, but which, if possessed by him in any degree, may be cultivated to great advantage. That is the capacity to govern large bodies of men, so that they shall feel that not only are they in the hands of one who knows more than they, but also of one who, with firmness, combines placability and justice.

This is a *resumé* of the requirements which are looked for in the locomotive superintendent. He is master of the situation, and, like the heads of all the departments, is equal to all emergencies. A man who has drawn his experiences from so many and varied sources, cannot fail, with natural gifts, to illuminate his position, and perform the functions of his office with acceptance to his company and credit to himself. The two great divisions or sections of his departmental duties are the *out-door* and the *in-door*. Of these he takes a general supervision, leaving the working-out of details to trained assistants. We are aware that on some of the greater lines, such as the London and North-Western and the Midland, the former of whom construct their own engines, carriages, and waggons, and both of whom have an unusually heavy account of rolling stock, it has been found expedient to still further divide the responsibility, and to separate the care of looking to the maintenance of engines from that of carriages and waggons. These, however, are not examples of the *general* division of the duties of the office, and we prefer to look away from these exceptional cases to the *common* practice. In the *out-door* section the superintendent has control of the running of all trains, passenger, goods, and mineral. He is consulted by the heads of the traffic departments in all train arrangements in order that he may provide engine-power to work the traffic. He arranges his engines so that the best and most powerful shall be promptly in their places for the express passenger, and goods trains, manned by the steadiest and most experienced drivers and stokers. He keeps a staff of cleaners constantly in the running sheds, with a squad of practical workmen, to see that the engines are in proper condition, both as to cleanness and repair, before driver and stoker remove them. He arranges that coaling and watering are fully attended to, that an adequate supply of sand, oil, and waste are provided for the journey, and also that the driver and stoker are in their places, and sober enough to occupy them. In addition to the express trains, he finds engine-power for all other main line and branch trains, for piloting purposes, for shunting operations in the chief passenger and goods termini, and, where it can be managed, he has a reserve of engines at certain points of the system for cases of emergency. These he mans from the running sheds with his best available resources. It is no easy matter to supply every demand from all quarters, and yet keep down train and shunting mileage, yet *that* is one of his special causes of worry. Equally difficult is it to maintain economy in the employment of necessary material, and an efficient staff at a minimum cost, in the presence of strong competition. In this *out-door* department of his work he is assisted by professional men who are training for the first places. His principal assistant is an engineer who knows the practical part of the work, and can manage the details as his deputy. This assistant must have a capacity for organisation, as with him must rest the management of the running staff. He must know what engines are available, and who are the most reliable drivers and stokers. He will have the task of working the trains, of arranging that the engines shall have full loads out and back again, of timing them and recording the day's work of each. He will be charged with taking precautions against the chance of coals or coke running short at coaling stations, of seeing that all needful stores are kept in proper quantity, and of testing the men as they come forward for promotion. In this matter he has to pass cleaners to the rank of firemen and drivers, first on mineral and shunting, then on goods, and ultimately on passenger trains. In order to this he requires to know what is necessary in a driver—capacity to read various styles of handwriting, so that he may readily read the orders posted up, from time to time, for his instruction, in the running shed; knowledge of the signals and whistles; discrimination of colour, that he may easily and accurately distinguish the various signals at night; and he must be able to test a man's capacity for working his engine, and for setting it to rights, by the way, in any number of possible cases of disaster. This assistant will have the control of foremen of the running sheds, and of the coaling and piloting stations, and also will direct the movements of the inspectors in their various districts. In addition to this, he will control the office staff, keep careful registers of work, stores, orders, a staff-book, &c., and conduct all correspondence. With such and so many various cares upon his head one would think the locomotive superintendent would have enough to do. His assistants, of all grades, lighten his hands of details, yet the whole responsibility devolves upon him; he, alone, will be called upon to excuse blunders, irregularity, or increased expenditure, and these demands upon his mental resources must inevitably tell upon him, unless he is a man of iron constitution. We have yet another, and equally harassing section of his work to notice, however, a glance at which will satisfy the reader of the heavy charge which is laid upon the locomotive superintendent.

The *in-door* department which has to do with the mechanical genius of the man, and exercises it in construction, reconstruction, and repair of plant, is that, no doubt, upon the wise and creditable administration of which our locomotive engineer plumes himself most. The *out-door* department may be administered by a good practical man with a capacity for organisation and the management of men, and need not call for fine-spun theories. Indeed, many such men have in the history of the service attained to honourable distinction in that department. In the *in-door*, however, the case is entirely different, none but a professional mechanic *can* undertake the responsibility; and this will readily appear. Even if we leave out of sight the necessity of *construction* we have that of *reconstruction*, or the removal of important, but worn-out parts of engine plant, and their replacement by absolutely new and sometimes improved parts. None but an expert could design, and, in designing, alter and improve upon the worn out. Without such knowledge and skill, a knowledge of the requirements and a skill in adapting that knowledge, which could only be gained by graduated experience, failure and disgrace would follow the attempt. Not only must there be *design* in planning the reconstructed parts, there must also be careful selection of suitable material. That selection must be in the mind of the engineer in designing. He has to specify the measurement, form and quality of the materials, to calculate strain, to satisfy himself theoretically that the parts will, when fitted together, perform the work intended safely and satisfactorily. Even when his design is on the exact lines of the portion to be replaced, he has to consider the question of piecing *new* materials upon the old, of fixing a new barrel upon an old stock, of putting new wine into old bottles. Theory and practice go hand in hand here, and assist him in determining whether extensive and radical replacements are safe, or even possible, in some cases. Whether an engineer is entrusted with the *construction* of his own engines, or has to contract for them, the work of design and specification equally devolve upon him. A knowledge of the requirements of the traffic will guide him as to size and strength. It will also affect his adoption of a certain class of stock, one class being suitable for express goods and passenger trains, another for ordinary main line, and another for branch line traffic (shunting engines are frequently second-class or partially used up, and repaired, engines). A distinct proof of the practical capacity of our locomotive engineers is to be found in the great diversity of design exhibited among the companies. Each man has his own special theories, and endeavours to embody these in the build of his own plant. Indeed, the decease or retirement of one man has not seldom led to something like a complete revolution in the style, character, and capacity of that company's rolling stock, his successor, with a wider experience, being anxious to adopt improvements out of a livelier sympathy with growing needs. The history of the development of the locomotive, since its infancy in George Stephenson's time, is a history as glorious and honourable to the inventive and unresting genius of our locomotive engineers as any which will ever be emblazoned on any page, and that genius was never at a *whiter heat* than at the present time. We have spoken of *construction* and *reconstruction* as important and leading functions of the locomotive superintendent in the *in-door* department. In endeavouring to estimate the professional value of that officer's services, it seems unnecessary to distinguish between these leading functions—they appear to us as practically indistinguishable. If he does not construct or build, he *designs*, and he designs as one who *could* build if need be; while, as we have shown, there are so many initial difficulties—in grafting new materials and new designs upon old materials and old designs—that the conclusion is driven home upon us that efficient reconstruction is as severe a test of capacity as construction. Besides engine plant, there are carriage and waggon stock to be provided and efficiently maintained. These also may be built in the company's shops—they *are* in the shops of some of the larger companies—or they are let out to contractors. In any case they have to be designed, and these designs are constantly being improved upon. This also is the work of the locomotive engineer, who, if he is not himself an inventor, must be abreast of anything known of the nature of improvement. Except in the matter of internal fittings, there is considerable uniformity of design in carriages. We do not, of course, shut our eyes to the recently introduced Pullman parlour and sleeping cars, or the varieties of sleeping cars adopted on the long routes. Nor do we thrust out of notice the many varieties of brake power at present on trial. Still, with all this before us, we think we are correct in saying that there is considerable uniformity of design in the construction of our carriage stock, and we think that is well. Our common carriage is British in design, and seems suited to our insular prejudices, and uniformity does not therefore mean paucity or sterility of invention. With such work, then, as that of the construction and reconstruction of engines and carriages, to say nothing of waggons, which demand much thought, the locomotive engineer has his hands full. Manifestly he requires assistance, and that of a professional class. He can only *indicate*, in many common instances, the leading idea to his chief draughtsman, and leave him to work out the details of design. He cannot be his own foreman of the erecting, fitting, machine, forge, boiler-making, smith, pattern-making, carriage-building, trimming, painting, and saddler's shops. These sectional operations must be entrusted to specially skilled workmen, and these, again, must be personally supervised by a chief mechanical assistant, who, with the chief designer or draughtsman, should possess qualifications of the same order as the superintendent, else their assistance would be a source of weakness. On extensive systems it is always necessary to have shops for repairs at certain great centres and distant termini. These are usually governed by an assistant superintendent or superior foreman, who can be trusted with the needful work of repairs, both trivial and important, and who has the faculty of administration. At junctions with other companies, at important junctions on his own line, and at stations at certain distances apart, there are also stationed, under the control of the chief of the nearest repair shop, a staff of inspectors, whose duty it is to examine all carriages and waggons passing their junctions, and to send the broken-down or the invalided to the hospital, with their indication of what is needed legibly chalked upon them.

In these days, when labour and capital are so constantly waging war, and workmen are combined in trades' unions for their mutual protection, the locomotive superintendent, who is, practically, an extensive employer of labour, has a rough and unenviable time of it, and had needs be a man of a peaceable and genial disposition if he would steer himself clear of difficulties. We have said that suavity with firmness is a grand qualification. It is nowhere more frequently called into active exercise than in administering the office upon which we have been enlarging, and it is creditable in the highest degree to the gentlemen who hold that office on our various systems that conflicts are of comparatively rare occurrence.

Apprentices to the profession are received on all the lines. There is great variety in the mode of receiving them. Many pay premiums; the majority do not. But *all* must pass the probation of the shops— the more thoroughly in earnest pass to the drawing office—graduate in mechanics, algebra, and mathematics, and if they are ambitious, apply themselves, during their leisure, to all collateral study.

CHAPTER IX

THE STORES DEPARTMENT.

THE *stores department*, the next in the order of survey, is the *commercial* arm of the service, and the chief store-keeper, or stores superintendent, is perhaps the only officer in the service whose principal qualification is that of merchant. He needs no special *railway* experience, and yet he can be trained nowhere else. An American general store, where everything "from a needle to an anchor" may be procured, seems to our mind the nearest approach to a training-ground, yet, transplanted from that likely soil to a railway store, the would-be storekeeper would find himself confronted by multitudinous difficulties, for overcoming which he had no ready resource. No great commercial undertaking, however extensive the range of its operations, and no branch of the public service makes such a variety of demands upon its leading spirit as this department of railway enterprise; and we hope to show, by an examination of some of the details, that it is perhaps the most interesting of the many departments into which railway management is divided. We are aware that the practice of the companies in the purchase and distribution of stores is dissimilar. In our treatment of the subject, therefore, it is likely that no two companies will recognise an exact picture of their special *modus operandi*. We think it better, for the information of the uninitiated, to describe a stores department in which every conceivable requisite for railway working may be found in stock, or through which every department is supplied with these.

When a line of railway is projected, as everyone knows, its construction is contracted for, the contractor finding all necessary material. Immediately it is opened for traffic the company owning it begins to be responsible for the supply of everything needful for working that traffic. It procures all classes of rolling stock, engines, carriages, vans (luggage, brake, meat, and fish), waggons, &c., of their several classes and capacities.

Then the labours of the stores superintendent commence. Engines will not move without coal, oil, and grease. They cannot be coaled without shovels, oiled without tin vessels from which to drop the oil, or greased without the grease-pan and the stick. The driver must have tools for the accidents incident to constant running, nor can he keep his fire-box clean without rakers, or his oily machinery sweet and in a condition favourable to smooth working without "waste." When an engine goes into hospital for repair, the locomotive foreman at the "running shed" cannot set it up again without lengths of brass tubing, fire-bars, castings of various forms, nuts, bolts, screws, sheet-iron, brass, valves, cocks, &c., and he cannot, if he possesses all these in abundance, make any use of them without the needful tools. When carriages are put upon the traffic, they also must be greased and their wheels tapped at the principal stopping stations, and the tapping calls for a special hammer. In the daily traffic, carriages require exterior washing, and that implies the need of pails and brushes—not to speak of water— which, however, it is never the duty of the stores department to supply. Unfortunately for the companies— though fortunately for workmen and the manufacturers—carriage plant *will* deteriorate. The cloth covering and cushions wear, become greasy, or get cut into holes, and need repair. Without fine cloth or leather for the first, and coarser for the second or third class, these repairs cannot be performed. Buttons and binding are in constant requisition, new leather straps for the windows, new blinds, and now and again new glass. The parcel racks get out of repair and call for new netting or new rods; the clean, light leather cloth covering the pannelling, or the gilt beading, becomes the worse for wear, and must be replaced; so must the carpet with the company's motto and crest; and the perforated matting for the smoking compartment will not last for ever. Frequent tossing about from roof to platform, that is, from the roof to the hands of the lampman on the platform, and much rough usage in the lamp-room, tells, sooner or later, on the whole fabric of the roof-light, and the glass globes get broken, the tinned work battered out of shape, and the brass and iron mountings worn or destroyed. A much enduring British public will not sleep in the dark on a night journey on that account, however, and repair or replacement follows damage or destruction. The exterior of the carriage has its demands on constant attention also. It is first to sustain injury in accident. If the whole fabric is not smashed in disastrous collision,

THE STORES DEPARTMENT. 75

panels are split or crushed in, door-handles are wrenched off, footboards are torn away, springs, wheels, or axles, couplings, chains, drawbars, or buffers are broken, or, in the ordinary wear and tear of everyday use these latter give way, as does the paint, this last with frequent washing. When a carriage goes into the repair shop for any or all of these repairs, there must be a supply of everything requisite, a handy accessible stock of needful materials. A different class of material is wanted for the repair of goods and mineral waggons, coarser and stronger, and more bulky as stock in store. Timber, bolts, spikes, screws, nuts, heavier springs and axles, stronger drawbars, chains and couplings, coarser paints, &c., while waggons constructed to carry long timber and bar iron, cattle and sheep trucks, horse boxes and fish vans, each demand the keeping of a stock of articles peculiar to each, when sent in for repair. The very tools required in the waggon repair shops, the running sheds, &c., are supplied, as required, from the store-keeper's stock. If the stores superintendent had nothing to do but provide all the material we have enumerated here, he might be admitted to have enough and variety of responsibility. His view is not bounded by the rolling stock, however. He has a look out upon the permanent way. The elements and the constant passage of heavy traffic at high rates of speed combine to wear out rails, sleepers, spikes, bolts, nuts, keys, fishplates, connecting rods, and the machinery of the signal box, its levers, joints, chains, rods, &c. These are in constant demand at all points of the system, the gangs of surfacemen or platelayers on their several lengths being continually occupied in replacing the old and worn-out with fresh material. The very tools they use, their shovels, picks, hammers, crowbars, are supplied from the same inexhaustible source. Then the telegraph staff must be supplied with telegraph instruments batteries and chemicals therefor, with wire of various strength, insulators poles, and all needful tools for stretching or tightening and joining the wires, erecting the poles, &c. A special feature of the responsibility of the office of store-keeper, or stores superintendent, in connection with the provision of needful materials for the permanent way and telegraph departments, is that he is charged with the collection and care of all old, superseded material. We shall refer to this further on, however.

The particular stores department we have in view as we write supplies stations with hand brushes for cleaning carriage seats and sweeping carpets, brushes for sweeping the platforms, pails and mops for washing the outsides of carriages, chloride of lime for disinfecting water-closets, cattle trucks, and pens, dusters and washing cloths for waiting-room and office furniture and floors, oil or candles for the station signal lamps, clocks and telegraph instruments, and it contracts for the supply of time bills and other such posters. It supplies, repairs, and replaces station lamps, burners, reflectors, extincteurs, and all that is necessary to keep the station fire-engines in good repair and working order; and at terminal stations foot-warmers for the winter passenger traffic, tail-ropes, spare couplings, snibbles, screw-jacks, and all handy appliances for getting carriages and waggons that have left the metals into position again, are also drafted from the stores, together with rope and twine, and all such useful articles; and, of course, there is always a plentiful supply of grease, oil, and waste for the cleaners on the station staff, and soap and towels for the cleansing of the clerkly hands. Indeed, even in the matter of supply of office furniture, and its repair from time to time, the stores department is charged with the responsibility Waggon and lorry or van covers are also made and repaired by that active and many-sided department; while of course, books of all kinds, invoices, parcel way-bills, audit office and Clearing House returns, inaccuracy sheets, over and undercharge forms, memorandum forms, letter and note paper, envelopes, pens, ink, pencils, pins, rulers, ink glasses, indiarubber, blotting paper, brown paper, foolscap, tickets, luggage, game and fish labels, waggon labels, "engaged" and "smoking" labels, &c., &c., are provided from the same boundless stores. There is really no limit to the demands made upon the department; scarcely any branch of industry with which it has not intimate connection.

We have referred to a special stores department, which we have selected as possibly representative of the practice of the most extensive systems. In this special instance there is a large saw-mill in which timber of various kinds, in logs, is cut to all sizes for every conceivable purpose, the scraps being utilised for scotches, and other inferior purposes, or, when not available even for such, are cut into firewood for office use. There is also a tinsmith's shop, where the company employ a large number of workmen and apprentices in the manufacture and repair of foot-warmers, signal, station, platform, carriage, van, engine, and hand-lamps of all descriptions; reflectors, oil-cans, and other tin work of a miscellaneous character. Ten minutes in that shop are enough to deafen the unaccustomed for life, and yet the workmen hear each other speak!

But for the noise, a look round will interest even the stolid. We walked into the building where the grease for lubricating the axles is made. The process is interesting, but should not be witnessed before dinner. The odour emitted from boiling palm oil and tallow is not appetising. Still less is it conducive to the enjoyment of dinner to look through the sheet-shop and watch the process of coating the waggon covers, yet half an hour there will repay the inconvenient experience of nausea. We found huge bales of canvas being cut into lengths and sewed together firmly and rapidly at several leviathan sewing machines, propelled by steam, and should judge it was hot work. Boys were busy sewing in the brass and iron rings at the edges through which the fastening cord is passed when the covers are in use. In another part of the building an extensive floorage was occupied by men charged with mending used sheets. These parts of the building resembled a large sail loft. We were more interested in a new process for coating the sheets. It would serve no object to describe the machinery—for the process is one controlled and carried on by steam power—even if we were capable of or entitled to do so; suffice it to say that the machinery is simple. One engine supplies power to the coating apparatus, the preparation of the coating oil, and the sewing machines. When a cover is made it is sent to be coated. We follow it and find that the coating process consists of its being carried to a long table, alongside of which there is a long tank containing the coating material. One edge of the cover is passed under a rod lying on the surface of the tank. That edge is then fastened to a movable rod suspended horizontally over the table. The machinery is set agoing, and the cover is drawn tightly and strongly through the tank, and in descending is folded lengthways as it falls on the revolving table. It goes into the tank of a fair giraffe colour—it is folded lamp or coal black. The process does not occupy over two minutes, and it secures—much more than the old system of hand painting —a thorough saturation of the canvas. The cover thus blackened is then hung up to a lofty ceiling, the building being warm, and in a day or two is dry and ready for a second plunge in the " black broth "—to be folded and then hung up till dry enough to admit of stencilling the company's name and marks, and its consecutive number, upon it. In this sheet-shop there are upwards of 4,000 waggon, lorry, and cart covers made annually, requiring about 150,000 yards of canvas. The work is not *sweet*, as we have said, and it is not clean: the workmen's hands and arms are plunged continually in a bath consisting of oil, lamp-black, and other such ingredients, which, if cooling in hot weather, as probably it is, requires hot water and soap, with a little persistent friction, to remove its traces. Another interesting but not too pleasantly odorous operation, conducted under the care and supervision of the stores superintendent, to whom we have already referred, is that of creosoting timber. Sleepers would not live out half their days, nor would telegraph poles stand up for themselves so independently if they were not carefully waterproofed before being used. Creosoting has been proved the best choke-damp, and the company in question, with some others, have undertaken the experiment of creosoting their own sleepers and telegraph poles, and each with some measure of success, although the time, in their experience, has scarcely arrived when a decided opinion may be offered as to the financial value of the experiment of performing this work themselves. We looked in at the works, and were at once seized by the nose, not by the manager or his assistants, but by the creosote fumes, which are very pungent. Around us on every hand were piles of fresh sleepers, and yet fresher were being unloaded from scores of waggons. The process of creosoting was new to us, and possibly may be so also to most of our readers, so we shall not apologise for describing it shortly. In the first place, creosote oil is laid in in tanks under the ground level. Large air-tight cylinders, made of stout boiler plates, and of the form of an elongated egg, opening at both ends, are placed conveniently to the tanks; there is an engine at hand communicating with the cylinders and the tanks; the cylinders are filled tightly with sleepers or poles, the ends are closed and screwed firmly, the engine pumps out all air from the cylinders, sucks out all moisture from the pores of the wood, and then, having produced a vacuum, the opening of a valve in a communication from the tanks affords a passage for the oil, which is sucked in till, filling up all available space, it ceases flowing, and the operation is almost at an end. The oil in this way not only covers the surface of the timber, but is literally forced by a natural law into the vacant pores. The workmen then unscrew the bolts in the ends of the cylinders, throw the doors open, and proceed to discharge them. Then it is seen that the timber, the last staves of which but half an hour ago you saw built in dry and clean, has been not only coated but literally *packed with oil*, and is, in all likelihood, thoroughly "impervious to damp and internal decay." We were told that if the timber is fairly dry it takes but *three hours* from the charge to the discharge of the cylinder, as many as from 450 to 500 sleepers being creosoted in that time in each cylinder. If the sleepers have not been thoroughly seasoned before the process, it takes longer to expel the moisture and prepare for the ingress of the oil. This will be manifest to our readers. We stood for some minutes at one end of a cylinder while it was being discharged, and were warned not to risk a longer exposure to the fumes, as they have the effect, when escaping from their confinement, of attacking the skin of the unaccustomed and making it *smart* violently. We were also warned against treading on the creosoted timber, or on the ground in its immediate vicinity, lest we should carry away the odour to diffuse it unwelcomely in the railway carriage, the office, or the parlour at home. The workmen change their clothes every time they leave work.

We have thus shortly endeavoured to show the range of the stores superintendent's duties and responsibilities, by describing the indebtedness of *all* departments to his arrangement and forethought. No railway work can be performed without his aid. All departments are dependent upon his watchfulness and readiness. Walk through the labyrinths of his repository, and say what you *cannot* find there. We could fill a few pages with a bare list of the articles lying on his shelves. All kinds of permanent way materials and tools, locomotive materials and tools, waggon and carriage materials and tools, telegraph materials and tools, candles for signals, soap and soap powder, sponges, clocks and watches, india-rubber goods, crucibles, fittings for signals, spelter, tin, and lead, spring balances, steam gauges, office and waiting room furniture, carriage fittings and trimmings, cloth for uniforms, drysalteries, gas and water fittings, glass goods, grain sacks, lamp furnishings, locks for carriages, desks, drawers, &c.; lamp-wick cottons, pressure gauges, grindstones, oils for lubricating and burning, for paints, and for creosoting purposes; ropes, cordage and twine, dressed flax, baskets, felt, varnishes, timber, coals, coke, ironmongery, matches, needles, dressing-combs, blankets, water columns, injectors, safes, stationery of all conceivable kinds and qualities, &c., &c., &c. These are but a few of the wares you will find displayed in a most orderly chaos on the rows of shelves, or stacked in the spacious timber yards and iron stores. Look in upon the heads of departments and see how carefully the stock books are kept: not a pound of goods or a yard of material comes in or goes out without a careful debit and credit entry, so that a reference to any of these books at any moment reveals at a glance the quantity on hand of any article, and warns the stores superintendent when and what to buy. We have referred to the item of cloth for uniforms as among those kept in stock. We have seen bales of cloth—superfine, for station-masters, guards, and inspectors; pilot, for goods and mineral brakesmen, and corduroy for porters and pointsmen—together with uniform caps of all kinds. We were carried from the raw material to the tailor's shop, where something like 30 men were discovered busy at work, making up uniforms of all classes, shapes, and sizes, and were told that that was the permanent staff of tailors. Uniforms are only delivered once a year, but almost everything else is in constant demand. Contracts are made annually with merchants and manufacturers for the supply of goods special to them, the stores superintendent having previously satisfied himself as to the utmost of his possible requirements in all branches. Should the quantity contracted for be less than that needed, he knows he must buy further at the market price then ruling; if more, he must keep it in stock till wanted. There are several items for which he cannot find room, demanding a larger stock than will suffice for a few months' need, such as coal, coke, timber, and rails. These, moreover, fluctuate so much in price that it is rarely expedient to make long contracts. For these the stores superintendent must, therefore, be frequently in the market, and he needs be a shrewd observer of daily prices to know when to buy. In all his dealings with the merchants and manufacturers his capacity is severely tested. None of them claim a tithe of his knowledge of *everything*, but each is a *specialist*. To be a successful purchaser, to be able to meet them all, he must know not only *something* of everything he buys, but so much of everything as will enable him to buy wisely. He must be a judge of both quality and price. What buyer in the largest of our mercantile establishments is required to profess a knowledge so diffuse? The stores superintendent we have taken as our sample is not only this capable merchant, this wise and careful caterer for every want of the railway system, he is also a practical analytical chemist, keeping for reference and for comparison a sample of every article contracted for, and a correct record of its whereabouts when wanted. He is able to bring almost every product purchased to an infallible chemical test, detecting by that means the *shade* of inferiority of a spurious article, and demonstrating that to a certainty. His laboratory is his touchstone for fabrics and metals alike, and by means of it he has sharpened his mercantile wits. The knowledge that he *can* test the materials he purchases, and is, therefore, not easily duped, has helped to narrow the circle of his contractors to those who wish to do honest business.

The stores superintendent not only *buys* for the railway company of which he is a most invaluable officer, and distributes to the various departments what they require to their several orders—he also *sells*. All old materials—permanent way, locomotive, and telegraphic—are collected by, or sent in to him, and he, watching the market, must judge of the best time to dispose of these. Such is a short and somewhat meagre account of the duties and responsibilities of the stores superintendent. He is a veritable admirable Crichton. It is not every man who combines in himself so many high qualities—the quality of the merchant, the chemist, the almost omniscient administrator. The man who serves the office efficiently is possessed of qualities of mind of a high order, and is worthy of high consideration. His chief assistant has a splendid field for observation and practice, and the heads of departments should store up their experiences. If these may not all be stores superintendents, they may become invaluable, because methodical book and storekeepers.

CHAPTER X.

THE ACCOUNTANT.

HITHERTO we have been considering, with one exception (the secretary's department), the offices and the men in which and by whom the out-of-door's work of our railways is administered. Now we come to another important arm of the service, without which it would be impossible to get along. If a company, in the management of its business, went on incurring debt, or paying away its revenues without keeping books, it requires no expert to see that bankruptcy and ruin must ensue. There must be a book-keeper and books. There must be accurate balancing of profit and loss, and that on some well defined principle. The duties of station masters are not confined to the attendance upon passengers, the encouragement of traffic, by civility and attention, the ordering and disposing of the staff. There must be booking of passengers and goods, and the collection of cash, and the due and regular accounting for intromissions. Returns are therefore made to the audit office at stated intervals, and equally regular though more frequent transmission of cash to the company's treasury. These financial concerns are, directly, under the control of the company's traffic auditor, who is, to that extent, one of the company's book-keepers. This, though an essential and highly necessary and important feature of a company's accounting, has, however, to do only with its revenues, its receipts. The expenditure, or that which must be set against the profits of working, in arriving at the amount divisible among the shareholders, comes within the special oversight and care of the company's accountant, who, in order to give an accurate account of the actual profits during each half-year, must be supplied with every information affecting receipts and expenditure, from every source. No item of the company's finance may be withheld from him. No secret is too sacred to be entrusted to his keeping. He is responsible for accuracy to the shareholders and the *State*, and want of diligence in the fulness of his investigation or care in the acceptance of information supplied to him, may be visited upon his head by the strong and impartial hand of the law. He certifies the half-yearly statements of accounts, and must justify the balance he strikes before independent auditors, who will not be cajoled by mere assertion, but must satisfy themselves of the strictest accuracy.

A company's accounts are divided under the two great general headings of *capital* and *revenue*. The *capital* account embraces the capital authorised to be issued under the sanction of the company's various Acts of Parliament. Generally speaking, the capital consists of stock, and shares, and loans on debenture or debenture stock. It may be interesting to some of our readers if we step aside at this point and describe the difference between the several classes of capital, and the mode of their creation and issue. A company's *first* creation is usually that of *shares*, the nominal value of which is fixed at the date or time of their creation, and may vary, according as is resolved, from £10 to £50 per share. In the case of new companies the shares are offered to the general public with a likelihood of those who are locally interested taking them up. If a company is already in existence, and is creating and issuing new capital, allotments of the new shares are offered, in the first place, to present shareholders in rateable proportion to their holdings of the company's ordinary stock, and under such conditions as to price, whether at premium or par, and the amount of the first call as the company's position and the state of the money market may warrant. The allotment letter indicates the date beyond which the option of acceptance of shares lapses. Up till that date those who intend taking up their lots pay to the company's bankers the amount of deposit per share, and are, thereafter, registered in the company's books as the holders of these shares. In some cases the shareholder prefers paying up in full at once, receiving interest on the amount paid in advance, and also saving the worry and anxiety of calls of uncertain amount at uncertain periods. Care requires to be exercised in the registration of shares, and in the registration of deeds of transfer, that the proper consecutive numbers are noted, as it is not enough that a man be registered as the holder of so many shares, the certificate must bear the particular numbers, otherwise buying and selling and transfer would be next to impossible. This is, however, too obvious to need urging. When the shares are fully paid up, it is often expedient to consolidate them into stock, which renders them less troublesome to the holder, be he buyer or seller, and also to the company. For the purpose of consolidation, which is simply the grouping of ten £10, five £20, or two £50 shares into £100 stock, it is necessary, under the provisions of the "Companies' Clauses Act," that the shares shall be *fully paid up*. Three-fifths of the shareholders present at a general meeting, of which due statutory notice has been given, may then authorise the work of such consolidation. Certificates bearing that the holder of so many shares, numbered consecutively and particularly, is now the owner of *stock* in relative proportion to the nominal value of his shares, are thereafter issued, and these stock certificates cancel and render void the paper which each shareholder previously held of the company. Holders of stock may sell in the market through recognised members of the Stock Exchange, but the price received for the stock is regulated by various circumstances from day to day, such as the company's present position or its immediate prospects, the condition of the money market, or the operations of speculators on the Exchange. A man may get, as in the case of some of the best railway properties, as much as £140 to £150 for his £100, or, as in the case of less fortunate companies, he may get so low as £60, or even under that amount. The companies neither reap advantage from the premium prices, nor disadvantage from the prices which are below par—par being the term for stock at its nominal value. In either case the stock is a £100 stock, and the holder entitled to dividend on that amount.

The raising of capital under these heads involves the keeping of separate accounts in each shareholder's name, and of a register of mortgages and debenture stock, with an entry for every bond and debenture stock holder. In the case of the more extensive companies, these books are kept by the registrar, but in many cases the accountant is charged with their management. In any case, the latter officer deals with the aggregate debit and credit of these accounts as an element of his half-yearly balance of the company's financial position.

The capital thus raised is expended on the lines and works for which Parliamentary powers were asked and received, and the accountant's office is the centre to which all details of that capital expenditure are sent for manipulation. These are there classified under such general headings as "Lands and Works," which comprise all expenses incurred in the construction of the lines and working stock, which latter includes all plant.

The completion and opening of the parent line or new branches involve the opening of the *revenue* account. This account is credited with the receipts derived from all sources in working the traffic on the one hand, and debited with all expenses incurred on the other, the balance at the credit of the account at the end of the half-year being the profit divisible among the shareholders.

The *capital* and *revenue* accounts, and also the company's balance sheet, are made up half-yearly according to forms prescribed by the "Regulation of Railways Act, 1868," and are audited and certified by independent auditors appointed to the duty by the shareholders. In their certificate these gentlemen must declare that, having carefully scrutinised the accounts prepared by the accountant, and certified by him, they find them contain a full and true statement of the financial position of the company, and that the dividends proposed to be declared are *bona fide*, after charging the *revenue* of the half-year with all expenses, which, in their judgment, ought to be paid thereout. These half-yearly accounts contain, in the first-place, a statement of "Capital authorised and Created by the Company," detailing the various acts; and the amount of *capital* authorised to be raised under authority of each. In the second place, a statement of "Stock and Share Capital Created, showing the proportion received." This is made up from the company's principal ledger, and shows the aggregate amounts received from shareholders on account of the stock or shares created, the amounts, if any, of calls in arrears, and the amount of the shares uncalled, with the amount unissued, if any part of the total nominal value of the shares remains to be called up, or any of the total number of shares created remains to be issued at the date to which the accounts are made up. In the third place a statement of "Capital raised by Loans and Debenture Stock"—showing the amounts received at the end of the half-year immediately preceding, classified under the different rates of interest payable—and, similarly, the amounts at the date of accounting, and the difference, either increase or decrease, during the half-year. In the fourth place, the accounts show the "Receipts and Expenditure on Capital account," as made up from the principal books of the company, all of which are kept by the accountant. On the credit side of this account we have the total amounts received on shares and loans, and these, together with any other capital receipts, if any, not included in the statements just referred to, constitute the *capital* receipts of the company. On the debit side we have the expenditure, showing separately, that on lines open for traffic, on lines in course of construction, and on working stock, &c., &c., and the balance, if on the debit side, as will at once appear, shows the amount of expenditure in excess of receipts, or, if on the credit side, it shows the amount of receipts in excess of the expenditure—a happy state of affairs for the company. In the fifth place, a statement giving "Details of Capital Expenditure." These details are classified under the following heads, viz.:—"Land and Compensation," which includes the amounts paid to landed proprietors for land purchased, for lines and works, and to their tenants for loss and damage to crops, &c.: "Construction of Way and Stations," which includes the amounts paid for engineering, for construction, and, generally, for rails, chairs, sleepers, and all expenses incurred in the formation or construction of the line and stations: and "Law Charges, and Parliamentary Expenses, &c.," which includes all expenses not embraced under the other two heads. In the sixth place there is given a "Return of Working Stock," showing, under classified headings, the number of locomotives, carriages, waggons, and, generally, the number of vehicles used in the working of the traffic and owned by the company at the date of accounting. This statement is, practically, a half-yearly inventory of the company's rolling stock, and it is made up from returns furnished by the locomotive superintendent, and other out-door officers in charge of the company's plant. The seventh statement is an "Estimate of further Expenditure on Capital Account," showing what is likely to be required to be expended on new works during the immediately ensuing half-year, and also how much may be estimated to be needed in subsequent half-years. This statement is made up from information supplied by the company's engineers and others. The eighth statement gives the "Capital Powers and other assets available to meet further Expenditure," and shows the amount of share and loan capital authorised but not created, the amount of calls in arrears, uncalled and unissued shares created, and any other *capital* asset which the company may possess available to meet their further requirements. These eight statements exhaust the *capital* account.

Next follows the *revenue* account, number nine of the half-yearly accounts being the statement with which it leads off. The items on the credit side of this account are made up from returns furnished to the accountant, chiefly by the traffic auditor, and these show the revenue from all sources during the half-year. The items on the debit side show the expenses incurred in working the line or in obtaining the revenue credited on the other side of that account. The expenses are classified under different headings, and show what proportion is chargeable to each department of the service, together with such other revenue charges as compensation paid to passengers injured on the line, and the aggregate of the sums paid for damage to goods in transit, parliamentary expenses, incurred in protecting the traffic from projected competition, by the opening of new lines and branches in connection with neighbouring systems of railway, rates and taxes, passenger duty, &c.

These items are still further detailed under *abstracts*, in statement number twelve, where they are sub-divided into the minor classification, cost of wages and materials incurred in working, and wages and materials expended in repairing, &c. The balance of the *revenue* account is carried to statement number ten, which deals with the *net revenue* account. On the credit side of this account is brought forward, if there be any, the balance from the previous half-year, the balance, already referred to, transferred from the *revenue* account, and any other special credits derived from the working of the line, but not credited to the *revenue* account. On the debit side of the *net revenue* account is shown any special items of expenditure applicable to revenue, but not included in debits to the *revenue* account as for working expenses, such as feu duties, and ground annuals, interest, &c. The balance of this *net revenue* account is the balance available for dividend, and is transferred to statement number eleven, which shows its proposed appropriation. Number thirteen is the *general balance sheet*, in which are set forth the assets and liabilities of the company at the time of accounting. Number fourteen shows the *mileage* worked, while number fifteen, the last statement supplied on the company's half-yearly statement of accounts, shows the *train mileage* run during the haf-year.

From the foregoing explanation it will be seen that all accounts of *receipts* and *expenditure*, and full statements of the company's liabilities, are sent to the accountant, who uses the materials as well for the purpose of preparing these half-yearly statements for distribution among the shareholders, as for the company's financial rectitude. The half-yearly statements of accounts are printed from the statements and the balance-sheet prepared by the accountant, and duly certified by the chairman and himself, after these voluminous documents have received the imprimatur of the auditors as correct. These accounts are issued by the secretary to each person whose name appears on the company's register of shareholders at the time of closing that valuable record; and a copy must also, under a provision of the "Regulation of Railways Act, 1868," be forwarded to the Board of Trade, while the company are held under obligation to give a copy on application "to any person holding shares, or mortgage, or debenture stock, or bonds of the company."

A company's expenditure, being more particularly under the control of the directors, is that which devolves the greatest amount of labour upon the accountant's department. Generally, it comprises accounts incurred to contractors for work done, to merchants for materials supplied, and to tradesmen and others for repairs and furnishings, &c.; salaries and wages paid to the company's officers and servants, rates and taxes, interest, &c. These all fall to be dealt with in the office of the accountant, and to be so classified in the company's books as to facilitate the supply of information to the directors when asked for, and for the preparation of the published accounts in the form prescribed by Parliament. The amounts due to contractors for works are certified by the company's engineers—those due to merchants for materials supplied are certified by the stores superintendent; while those due to tradesmen and others are certified by the heads of the departments on whose account they are incurred. The salaries and wages' bills are made up and certified by the heads of departments. These, and all certified accounts, are sent periodically to the accountants department, where they are thoroughly examined, compared with contracts as to prices, &c., calculations checked, and abstracts of them made for submission to the board or the finance committee for instructions as to payment. They are then handed over to the treasurer or chief cashier, by whom they are paid, the payments being entered by him in a blotter or scroll cash book, which, with the vouchers, or receipts, are sent to the accountant; the payments to be recorded in the company's principal books, and the vouchers to be filed past for future reference.

The principal duty of the auditors is in the accountant's department, and the great business of the half-yearly audit is to see that *receipts* and *expenditure* are properly allocated to *capital* and *revenue*, so that the revenue balance shown to be available for dividend is not increased on the one hand by crediting in any way to *revenue* what should properly be credited to *capital,* or, on the other hand, by charging to capital what should properly be charged to revenue, and the ease with which the auditors may arrive at a full certainty as to this is dependent on the arrangement and the care bestowed on the book-keeping by the accountant and his staff. We know of one company, and doubtless there are many such, whose books and accounts are so arranged and so carefully kept that the auditors readily determine, to a certainty, whether the aggregate amount of debits and credits to *capital* and *revenue* respectively is the actual amount shown in the accounts proposed to be issued to the shareholders.

Besides keeping the accounts, the department is charged with the preparation of all financial statistics required by the Board of Trade, the statements furnished to the assessor of railways for valuation roll purposes, and those supplied to the income tax commissioners for purposes of taxation, and, generally, the preparation of all statements which in any way affect the financial concerns of the company.

In these somewhat voluminous observations, we have shown the quantity and character of the work devolving upon the company's accountant. There can be but one opinion of its supreme importance, and it needs but few words to show that the man who directs and controls a department with such responsibilities must possess certain valuable qualifications. There is perhaps nowhere outside of railway business so elaborate and intricate materials to manipulate. Certainly no merely commercial book-keeper, however long and varied his experience, could hope to be otherwise than confused among the multitudinous details of this department of railway business. It is like no other book-keeping system, except in its general principle. Nothing but long experience will impart familiarity with its details and cross entries. Hence the egregious blundering of men on 'Change and city editors, so frequently manifested in dissecting the published accounts of railway companies. Properly, to fulfil his high functions, the railway accountant should be an expert of experts in figures. Sound arithmetic, and a capacity to adapt its many rules to his emergencies, are necessary qualifications. A clear head and ready apprehension are equally invaluable. A knowledge of the special requirements of railway financing, and of the company's special powers and obligations as defined in its Acts of Parliament, and familiarity with the requirements of the Board of Trade, are not less cardinal requisites to an efficient railway accountant. He must needs be also an administrator, since much, indeed all, the detail work must be performed by his staff, who will require subdivision in departments, and careful instruction and supervision in the performance of their several duties. They will further, and as an elementary fact, require to be carefully selected and trained. The accountant must be a man of strict method, accustomed to work by rule and spirit-level, and, in this respect, his staff will insensibly follow him. His principal assistants must be such as he, in all these respects, and they must be careful and painstaking referees in all difficulties which stagger the members of the staff. Under such instruction and oversight young men of necessary capacity steadily grow like their officers, and are sensible, or the reverse if they do not profit by their training. Nothing proves so valuable in the character and qualifications of an accountant's clerk, next to neatness of hand and facility in figures, as the qualities of accuracy and perseverance.

CHAPTER XI.

THE TRAFFIC AUDITOR.

EVEN to the fully initiated, railway accounting often appears, as it in reality is, intricate and perplexing to a degree. Not even those primitive little lines, which, beginning nowhere and ending in no place in particular, and which are innocent of the complications of through booking, can be made to pay dividend without an amount of account-keeping which would seem to the outsider as almost inexplicable. It is not, however, our intention in this chapter to discuss the general question of railway accounting, which includes all the elaborate machinery called into play in order to strike the half-yearly balance between revenue and expenditure, between charge and discharge, and which results in the declaration of dividend. Of that we have treated in the last chapter. We shall here confine our attention to one special and distinct phase of the question—that, namely, of the *traffic audit*. And, first let us say, that by the traffic audit we mean simply the duties performed in the *audit office*. In some cases these duties are laid upon the accountant, and form a branch of his work. The audit office is so much more frequently separate and independent, however, that we prefer to treat it as if it were universally so, and we think that our readers will appreciate the separate treatment.

The Clearing House system has rendered it possible to book passengers, or to despatch goods, from Land's End to John O'Groats, at through rates and fares, the passenger or the trader having no need for worry about re-booking, and the various companies whose lines form the different links in the route being assured of their share of the profits of carriage. A most important factor in working this out is the traffic auditor, who is the medium through whom the Clearing House deals with the companies in matters of division of receipts. Booking and parcels clerks receive money in rates and fares, and give the passenger or trader certain rights and privileges over their company's lines, and, in the case of through transit, over connecting lines. The traffic auditor is, as a rule, advised of the receipts from these sources daily, by means of a copy of the cash note which accompanies the remittances to the bank, or to the company's cashier, and it is his province to see that these monies are duly accounted for. Goods agents or cashiers receive "porters'" collections, "*paid in*" freights, live stock and mineral charges, and they collect weekly or monthly accounts, on the one hand, and pay claims, "paid on" charges, &c., on the other hand, sending their cash to the bank or the company's cashier daily, supplying the traffic auditor with a copy of the cash note, and balancing the whole for that officer in the monthly balance sheet. The traffic auditor examines these statements of "charge" and "discharge" as often as he pleases, and as minutely as time and opportunity will admit. He is, practically, responsible for correct and regular accounting between the stations and the company, and is the only check upon carelessness or infidelity which the company possesses in traffic matters. He is a very wholesome check, because the radically dishonest cannot well escape detection, and, knowing that, are often kept in the narrow but safe and comfortable groove of uprightness, while the strictly scrupulous and careful find, in his periodical, or intermittent audit of their accounts, and his approving initials appended to each as it is examined, that confirmation of their conscious rectitude, and of their painstaking regularity, which is its own reward. We are far from saying that a thorough and capable audit of station accounts always succeeds in preventing dishonesty. The history of every company affords too frequent illustration that in spite of that care deception has been successfully practised. But we think it is due to the traffic audit, not merely to say that it has prevented deceit and fraud in thousands of possible cases, but it has the credit of *discovering* these in innumerable instances, and of bringing the guilty to justice. And it is impossible to believe that with ever-increasing experience, methods of station accounting will not one day be devised whereby the morally weak will be protected against themselves, and the work of the traffic auditor prove a yet more salutary check upon those holding positions of trust. When cases of incapacity or fraud are suspected a special investigation is made—by the audit office—and a report prepared for the goods manager, or the general superintendent and the general manager, in order that the person or persons concerned may be dealt with. When a station master, cashier, or booking clerk is removed, a special audit of the books is made, so that the new incumbent of either of these offices may have a clear start. When a new passenger station is about to be opened the traffic auditor hands over the necessary books and tickets to the newly appointed master, or, as in the case of superior stations, to the booking clerk, giving him all needful instructions, and taking his receipt for the property committed to his charge.

In the interests of his company, the traffic auditor is an observer of routes. When rates or fares are arranged between two competing companies for traffic which is to pass from one to the other company's system; and when these companies have more than one point of contact, or exchange for that traffic, the receipts are usually divisible between the companies by the most direct route. It sometimes happens that the sending company, however, in its natural zeal for its own interest, sends the traffic to the most distant junction, in order to secure, if possible, the longer mileage. Under a watchful audit this is not likely to be successful, however, as the department, being provided with a note of the arrangement, is certain to check the irregularity, and to insist upon a division by the shortest route. In connection with this, the traffic auditor is always provided with copies of agreements made between the company he represents, its competitors, and its allies. With the various clauses of these agreements he must make himself acquainted, in order that he may know his company's powers and obligations. A famous orator of a past age once declared in his place in the Imperial Parliament that he could "drive a coach and six through any Act" the legislature might pass. The saying was as true as it was witty, and it is as applicable to the work of our senators of the present day as to that of the days of the celebrated O'Connell. It is no less true of those documents so frequently scheduled to railway acts of our time, and called agreements; and it is perhaps still more true of those often less binding agreements which are executed between companies, or between any of these and their traders, or yet again between them and certain corporations for mutual advantage. We do not say that the ambiguity of terms used in Acts of Parliament, agreements, and such documents, is at any time *intended*. We charitably blame our copious English tongue which is so full of synonymous words and phrases that it is difficult to avoid the employment of some which may not mean exactly the same thing to everybody. One of the special difficulties which beset the path of the traffic auditor is the strict interpretation of debateable terms in traffic agreements, and this is a literary and legal test which proves the quality of the man. He is not, of course, left to read the riddle alone. He has probably had no share in the construction of its clauses, and no responsibility in its looseness of expression, consequently, he consults with the general manager, the goods manager, or the company's solicitor, and it may not unfrequently happen that, in his unclouded, unbiassed view, reading it for the first time, and free from the mental fatigue and strain of drafting it, he lets in a new light upon some faulty phrase which alters his company's position with respect to the agreement, to the apprehension even of its authors.

The traffic auditor has the adjustment of traffic accounts with leased companies, and with those whose traffic is worked by his own company—and that is always an onerous task, requiring much discretion and tact. He is also called upon from time to time to make up statements of traffic for the information of the Board—for the management, or for Parliamentary warfare. There is, we may observe, about the very air of the audit office a kind of *privacy* which seems to say "No admittance, except on business." The department is of the nature of a detective force whose operations none may know till the result is ascertained. This is true of its investigations, whether periodical or special. It is much more true of its care of the records of weekly traffic receipts. Possessing summaries of all kinds of traffic working over his company's lines, and being in constant communication with the Clearing House, the traffic auditor is in a position to indicate—once a week—by how much the gross receipts have increased or decreased in comparison with the corresponding week of the previous year. This he does in his traffic return. The eager waiting for these weekly publications, and the effect they have on the prices of stocks on "'Change," are matter of common observation, so that a speculating and investing public seem fully alive to the value of the information supplied through this important public medium, and no one will, therefore, fail to see that the utmost reticence is needed on the part of the officer who wields a weapon so dangerous. The problem of the week, about which there is so much breathless anxiety, must be worked out by the traffic auditor personally, or with the aid of a trusted assistant, lest many-tongued rumour, lynx-eyed and eavesdropping, should carry away even a hint of the secret before it is ripe for divulgence. Passenger tickets are issued from the audit office to the stations with a debit of their value; and, being treated as cash, they must be accounted for to the audit office. This arrangement includes season and traders', or composition tickets, together with tourist and pic-nic tickets, in their season. Parcels traffic, horses and dogs, with game and poultry—all are included in returns to the traffic auditor, and come under his cognisance; while the ticket collecting staff forward to his office daily all tickets, passes, &c., taken from passengers at their several stations.

This is a hasty review of the chief functions of the traffic audit; but it may be sufficient to indicate, in broad outline, the scope and requirements of the office. The man who would administer it thoroughly must needs be no stranger to railway work, and must be a fair accountant. There are many details of station accounting to which our space offers no opportunity of even referring; and, since the chief of the department charged with seeing that everything is carefully accounted for cannot be expected to investigate everything personally, it is obvious that he should know how everything is done, and advise in cases of complication. He cannot be too fully and broadly cultured—no officer can—and he should, as we have already indicated, specially be so fair a student of English as to be able to weigh the relative value of synonymous terms. We are speaking to our youthful aspirants to the office, well knowing that the present incumbents, in a majority of instances, illustrate our high ideal with many graces of capacity. Conscientiousness and industry are important qualifications, and cautious reserve is indispensable.

Such an office as the audit demands one chief assistant—one controlling head—one unfailing, trustworthy confidant. As in other departments, so here—this principal assistant should possess the same qualifications as his chief. If he have them not, he is like a broken reed—when most needed he fails. Where the traffic auditor is a man of the proper brand, his assistants have opportunities of improvement which only carelessness or incapacity would prevent them taking advantage of. Give us the *head* and we will prophesy as to the hands. The chief clerk, or principal assistant, coming most into contact with the head of the department, insensibly acquires style and tact from his association with his superior; and, if he be a sensible man, will be certain to discover through that very association the lurking ignorance with which the corners in his brain had been stuffed, and will gradually build up experiences of his own. Besides the principal assistant, there are heads of departments, the chief division of work in the office being goods and passengers. In the former the chief duty of the staff is to receive and check the abstracts or summaries of goods, live-stock, and mineral traffic, sent in from all stations; to record them; to pass them on to the Clearing House; and to correspond with the latter, and with stations in cases of discrepancy; and to see that the company's due proportion of the receipts is credited to it. There are minor details of work, such as the keeping of "rope" and "sack" accounts, the check of monthly balance-sheets, &c., which we need not do more than mention. The staff in this department has frequent interruption, in its monthly routine of work, in the constant demand for traffic statements, a kind of special duty which requires some care and more smartness There is also attached to the department a staff of travelling audit inspectors, who go now here, anon there, dropping down as from another sphere upon a station unawares, making investigation of books, and reporting upon outstandings and irregularities. In the passenger department the duties are as similar as the dissimilarity of the traffic will allow. There are the travelling auditors, making raid upon station masters and booking clerks, examining ticket stock and cash remittances; the office staff, taking account of station debits for tickets supplied, of station credits for tickets sold, advising the Clearing House by monthly abstracts or summaries of all foreign traffic, and taking care that the due division is credited by the latter, receiving and duly checking station summaries of parcel traffic, horses, carriages, dogs, game, and passenger live stock, recording the local and advising the Clearing House of the foreign, for mileage division of the receipts. This is, in brief, the work of the audit office. Its staff of clerks should be fair, accurate, and expert figurers. They have few opportunities of acquiring, in their routine duty, facility in composition, for the letters are chiefly routine and stereotyped. They have no chance of learning anything of the changeful out-of-door work of active railway management. There is a certain monotony about their daily labour which, at the first blush, is repellant; but to many mental constitutions there is a charm in figures, and their infinite capacity of involution, and the audit office has, therefore, an attraction for all such, which, allied with the consciousness that the work upon which they are engaged is second to none in the service in its importance, will always secure for it clever, clear-headed, and painstaking men, whose labours are worthy of fair remuneration. The travelling staff have responsible duties to perform, but should always discharge them with suavity, and we believe they are exemplary in that respect.

CHAPTER XII.

THE SOLICITOR.

The powers and privileges enjoyed by the railway companies are conferred, as our readers well know, by Parliament, in Special and General Acts passed from time to time. The Special Acts are applied for by the individual companies. The General Acts are usually promoted by Government "for the better regulation of railway traffic." These latter impose restrictive obligations "in the public interest," as the phrase is. Both classes of enactments affect the companies by defining their rights and by setting forth their obligations. It seems to be characteristic of the English language—not *specially* so, we believe— that many words and combinations of them are susceptible of such varied meanings as to render the work of the *Lawgiver* perplexing. We all know at least, that if a " coach and six " cannot be driven through an Act of Parliament, ingenious solicitors and counsel can find joints in the armour through which to attack a rival, or loopholes for escape from troublesome obligations. We do not think—as we have already said— that this ambiguity of expression in the Statute Book is intentional, though we *have* heard it broadly hinted that if the letter of the law were more simple and easy of comprehension, there would be fewer lawyers, and we know that the lawyers are the draughtsmen. We merely mention this rumour by the way, inclining rather to blame the many-tinted English tongue in which our laws are written; and nursing the belief that the legal profession feel aggrieved at the ambiguity of expression which perplexes their clients.

Well, it will be evident that companies possessing power and privilege in the conduct of their trade, sanctioned by special Acts of Parliament, and bound down by restrictions and obligations which, if neglected, may be punished, by appeal to the courts of law, cannot pretend to interpret the law for themselves without the aid of experts. Hence it arises that each has to call in professional assistance; each has to employ its own lawyer. Many of the companies appoint a duly qualified legal practitioner—in England and Ireland he is an attorney, in Scotland a solicitor—to the office of solicitor, who on his appointment resigns his general practice, and, becoming an officer of his company, devotes himself entirely to his company's interests. In some of the smaller companies it is the rule to call in the aid of some well known firm of attorneys or solicitors to advise on occasion. This latter course is, for the companies who adopt it, probably the cheaper and better one, as, from the small amount of legal advice and assistance they require, it would be more expensive to establish a solicitor and his assistants on their staff. For the greater companies, however, it is probably more expedient, and also less costly, to add a law department to the establishment. Everybody knows that "going to law" is a costly expedient, and well-advised people avoid it, when they can. Lawyers' fees are proverbially heavy, not intrinsically, but in their aggregate amount, as the profession knows how to protract a case, and heap on costs. Apart from great questions of policy, which turn up continually, and upon which, for the reasons given, it is necessary to have professional advice, there is a constant crop of trifling little matters in connection with claims, outstanding accounts, demurrage, rates and taxes, and such like, upon which the heads of departments require to have legal assistance. If the company merely hires that from a firm in business who will, very properly, charge for every such advice or consultation, those heads will consider well whether the advice is worth the expense, and probably decide for themselves, in equity, and oftentimes find themselves on the wrong side of an action in court. If on the other hand the company has a solicitor on the premises, that gentleman or his assistants will be appealed to in every difficulty, with the consciousness of getting what may fairly be presumed to be sound, responsible advice without cost or favour.

In this chapter we have to do only with the solicitor as the head of a department of railway business—a railway officer, in fact. It is necessary to his appointment that the solicitor be a duly qualified legal practitioner—that is, one who is qualified to practise the profession of law. He must be an experienced conveyancer, having all his company's landed interests under his charge. He requires to be familiar with the forms of procedure in Parliament, in the various courts, and in arbitrations. And it is essential, as a qualification for his office, that he should possess the readiness and concentration of thought necessary to grapple, at will, with such diverse matters as a mass of traffic returns, an engineering design, or a medical report. These are high and varied qualifications, and they place the railway solicitor on a loftier pedestal than his brother in general practice, for he must profess all that the latter knows and can do, *and much more.* The solicitor, as the company's legal adviser, often has a seat, with the general manager and the secretary, at the board. Equally with them, he is confidant of all the deep and hidden things of policy which are incubated at board meetings. He is versed in all the past, as he advises as to all the present schemes of the company, and he keeps a watchful eye upon the schemes of competitors. Not only so, to be useful, he makes it a point to master, together with his own company's statutory powers and obligations, those of neighbouring companies—allies as well as rivals. It is in his capacity as legal adviser on matters of policy that the railway solicitor proves his quality most. In the discharge of this important function he is consulted on all new schemes. If his company projects a new line, in the natural development of its resources, he must advise as to its possible interference with vested rights, public and private, and the likelihood of opposition. If the new scheme invades the territory of a competitor, he is expected to know whether the company is debarred by obligations to that competitor, and, if so, whether there is no loop-hole in any existing arrangements through which there may be a way of escape, and a chance of over-riding objection. This is, manifestly, a most invaluable function to be called upon to exercise. It is pleasant, when you have agreed with an adversary in black and white, to find, when it is convenient to do so, that you may discard the agreement because of some technical flaw. If there is no agreement debarring the invasion, it becomes his duty to forecast and anticipate the lines of his competitor's opposition, and to prepare for it. Having advised as to the feasibility of carrying a bill for the new scheme, he has nothing to charge himself with on the question of its desirability or necessity; his next duty is to carry the measure through Parliament. In this he is assisted by the general manager, who has to do with the policy of the scheme; by the engineer, consulting or resident, with whom rests the responsibility for the plans; and by a parliamentary agent in London, with whom he drafts the Bill. In connection with this, his assistants make up the necessary book of reference, which, with plans and other documents to be afterwards enumerated, must be lodged in the Private Bill Office of the Houses of Parliament, on or before the 31st day of December, in compliance with the standing orders of Parliament. The book of reference contains a description of the land or tenements, with a list of the owners, lessees, or occupiers thereof, proposed to be interfered with, and lying within the limits of deviation of the proposed line. From this book the solicitor's staff copies the requisite notices to owners, lessees, or occupiers, and these must be served upon each person affected by the scheme, on or before the fifteenth day of December. It is also necessary that, on or before the thirtieth day of November, he lodge with the proper officer of the county and township or burgh interested, a copy of the plans and sections, together with the relative book of reference, for inspection. Then he must prepare a list of *assents, dissents,* and *neuters* from the replies of those who are interested, *all* for lodgment, with the book of reference and plans, in the Private Bill Office of Parliament. There is also a list of the *labouring classes* who are to be dispossessed of their homes by the proposed scheme, to be prepared from the valuation roll, and the affidavits of those who have served notices require to be sworn to before the sheriff of the county, these affidavits proving that the *standing orders* have been complied with, and the *labouring classes* schedule must accompany the papers already referred to as requiring to be deposited in the private bill office already mentioned. We had almost omitted reference to the publication of notices in certain newspapers, including the *Gazettes* published in London, Edinburgh, or Dublin, as the case may be. These notices are drafted by the solicitor, and their publication is an essential part of the evidence of the *strictest* compliance with standing orders. The first stage of the Parliamentary proceedings is the passing of the bill by the examiners on standing orders, who, if they detect the slightest technical flaw, have the power to throw out the bill for the session on the very threshold of its progress. It will be evident from this that at no time dare the solicitor trifle with his preparations.

We must now assume that a Bill has passed to the House. The inexorable standing orders require that petitions against the Bill shall be presented within two, if in the House of Lords, and if in the House of Commons, within ten clear days after its first reading. The solicitor must look for these, and prepare his objections to the *locus standi* of the petitioners, if he has any to state. He must also not only have an array of witnesses ready, but he must have from each a precognition, or written statement, of what each is prepared to say in favour of the Bill. From these he prepares his brief for counsel, and the success or defeat of his application will depend mainly upon the character and quality of his case as indicated in the brief. Meanwhile there has been the appointment of a select committee of the House for the consideration of a group of Bills, our solicitor's among the number, with the naming of a day for the probable commencement of the hearing of each. According as his Bill is placed on the group will the solicitor's case come on sooner or later. He must be ready—often at a few hours' notice—to start for London with his witnesses and documents. Equally with the counsel and the Parliamentary agent, but with a far greater sense of responsibility than either, he must watch the case closely, putting forward or keeping back evidence according as he deems the exigencies of the case require. In hearing petitioners against the Bill, he has an especially difficult task to perform, as he knows nothing definitely, until he hears the evidence they are to offer. Then follow consultations with counsel and the Parliamentary agent as to how these witnesses are to be handled. The reader may feel sure that when a Bill *passes*, after so much high pressure, the solicitor has earned a rest with his laurels.

When the required Act has been passed, and the operations which it authorises are about to be begun, the solicitor prepares and adjusts the contracts—in the meantime let—under which the various portions of the work involved are to be undertaken. The proceedings for determining the amount of compensation to be paid for land and other property to be acquired, or interfered with, are conducted by him, and in many cases, where arbitration is necessary, he acts both as counsel and agent. In a great majority of instances the settlement of these claims is disposed of before an arbiter or arbitrators—appointed by mutual consent under the Lands Clauses Act. When the question of amount of compensation has been settled, it becomes the duty of the solicitor to *convey* the property to the company, and to have the company discharged of the claim. The *conveyancing* department of the solicitor's office takes cognisance of and investigates the title deeds, and prepares and adjusts —with the professional advisers of the sellers—the documents conveying the properties purchased from the seller by the company. As the sums of money expended from time to time in acquiring property or lands are necessarily great, it is always well to be satisfied that the property or lands are not burthened with mortgages, annuities, or other similar incumbrances, or to see that no title is accepted with a flaw in it. Carelessness in this, or a lack of professional skill, may involve heavy loss to the company. In this connection it is necessary to examine the whole of the titles with care, and to obtain from the public records corroborative evidence. This department also deals with all disputes arising with the feudal superior, with respect to his reserved rights in the land, and the annual or other periodical payments claimed by him on that behalf. It further adjusts all differences arising with co-terminous proprietors regarding boundaries and such matters. It may be well to state here that the solicitor has the custody of all the company's title deeds and muniments.

We have already hinted that the solicitor advises the traffic and other departments on all matters involving questions of law. He or his qualified assistants are at all times accessible, and, having such an adviser, the company is not, nor need ever be, at a loss to determine whether a claim for compensation for personal injury, or for loss of goods or market, is one which they ought to resist, or whether they have a good case against a trader for demurrage, a passenger for breach of bye-law, or against a trespasser on the line. The department which manages this branch of the company's solicitor's business is the writ or process department, and it looks after all court transactions. We need not say that this is a very onerous and exacting, and, too often, disagreeable part of the work of the solicitor's office. He cannot attend court personally, nor can his assistants, if, as in all large companies, the actions raised are numerous and in various courts. Where it is possible a qualified assistant appears in court for defence or prosecution, as the case may be; but in a large number of instances, it is necessary to call in the aid of local practitioners to look to the company's interest in special cases, these gentlemen receiving their briefs from the solicitor. The labour of getting up these petty cases is very great, and much skill and ingenuity is required, and the paucity of defeats in court in railway cases is a standing proof of the capacity of the solicitors' staffs. The public who raise the actions are often relentless, and it is not their fault if they do not prevail. Some very intricate cases arise, from time to time, in the superior courts, calling for much finesse in the management of witnesses drawn from all points of the compass, to speak to what appears, at first sight, trifling technicality. We have known more success than failure result from such skilful tactics. This department is invariably in the hands of a duly qualified assistant, a gentleman who, like his chief, is entitled to practise as a solicitor, and, if he is as industrious as his duties demand, he is a tower of strength to the head of his department.

The solicitor has his book-keeping department also, in which there is an accurate account kept of all the business done, and of all cash transactions, and through which all accounts for payments and all cash statements are checked and certified.

In the foregoing remarks we have endeavoured to give a short sketch of what is required of the railway company's solicitor, from which it will be seen that, while trained for a learned profession outside the railway preserves, he insensibly acquires a large railway experience, and becomes as thoroughly a railway officer as any of those who eat his company's bread. We have made out a strong case, we think, for establishing his title to be regarded as a very busy man; and we think, moreover, that he is entitled to be regarded as a most invaluable railway officer.

He cannot do everything himself, no matter what his intellectual and physical energy. He cannot even superintend every detail. The departments we have described are therefore placed under the charge of assistants, who, to ease him properly of detail must be trained and cultured as he has been, self-reliant, capable gentlemen, with ripe knowledge, and receptive, ready brains, accustomed to form dispassionate opinions, based on ample knowledge of the principles of law, and a genuine love for their profession. With such assistance the solicitor is free to be at the disposal of his brother officers in advising on weighty matters, and to be counsel and confidant, as we have said, of the board. With such examples before them, the juniors miss golden opportunities of improvement if they do not keep steadily bent on imitation.

www.ingramcontent.com/pod-product-compliance
Lightning Source LLC
Chambersburg PA
CBHW031419160426
43196CB00008B/992